"So helpful that many readers no doubt will tweet its praises and thank @timoreilly and @sarahm—the authors' Twitter handles—for helping people understand why Twitter is emerging as the Internet's most powerful communications vehicle since e-mail."

—Associated Press

"Tim O'Reilly and Sarah Milstein are two of my favorite tweeters, and they've just written *The Twitter Book*, a pleasingly-designed guide to making the most out of Twitter."

—Boing Boing

"The text is almost haiku-like, illustrated with example tweets. I think of it as a kinda Strunk and White for Twitter with brevity, wit, great examples, and simplicity."

—How Nonprofits Can Use Social Media

"An effective handbook towards setting up a cohesive and consistent identity on Twitter. "

—Galley Cat

"Provides clear advice to enlighten everyone, from the first-time tweeter to the power user."

—School Library Journal

"Manages to pack in all kinds of information of interest to Twitter virgins and aficionados alike.

—New Scientist Magazine

"Accomplishes what it sets out to do: To provide a clear introduction to both a powerful tool and the culture that has grown up around it. If you're interested in using Twitter for your business, this book is excellent. Strongly recommended."

—Web Marketing Today

"Tim O'Reilly and Sarah Milstein have written a book full of helpful hints on branding via Twitter."

—Examiner.com

"The most useful book we've seen on the topic to date."

—Design Tools Monthly

Praise for the first edition from Amazon reviewers (we don't know these folks!)

"If you're new to Twitter, this book will absolutely shorten your learning curve. If you've been using Twitter for a while, you will learn things you don't know but should."

—George A. Burks

"Whether you're an individual looking to build your own personal brand online, someone who is considering starting a business, or part of a large company, the book is chock full of ideas, resources, and helpful advice."

—Christa Avampato

"Twitter should PAY O'Reilly and Milstein for having written *The Twitter Book*....The book is LOADED with definitions, tips and tricks to make your Twitter experience a productive one."

—Manny Hernandez

"If possible, this book should be required reading when someone signs up for a new Twitter account."

—J.J. Kwashnak

"After finishing *The Twitter Book*, I now know more about Twitter and how to effectively use it. In fact, using O'Reilly and Milstein's book, I have actually begun to grow my business organically leveraging the information provided."

—Carla Fair-Wright

"If Twitter ever came up with their own official book, it is hard to imagine how it would be much different than this one. I highly recommend it to anyone who is interested in making the most out of their Twitter experience."

—Dr. Bojan Tunguz

"*The Twitter Book* is a great primer for anyone who wants to expand their network, supplement their job search or customer base, or make new friends and contacts."

—D.A. Allen

"I found this book a marvelous blend of form and function. Every question, big or little, was answered quickly, and I found myself putting unexpected functions to work smoothly."

—William Burden

SECOND EDITION

The Twitter Book

by Tim O'Reilly and Sarah Milstein

O'REILLY®

Beijing · Cambridge · Farnham · Köln · Sebastopol · Tokyo

The Twitter Book

by Tim O'Reilly and Sarah Milstein

Copyright © 2012 Tim O'Reilly and Sarah Milstein
Printed in Canada.

Published by O'Reilly Media, Inc., 1005 Gravenstein Highway North, Sebastopol, CA 95472.

O'Reilly books may be purchased for educational, business, or sales promotional use. Online editions are also available for most titles (http://my.safaribooksonline.com). For more information, contact our corporate/institutional sales department: (800) 998-9938 or corporate@oreilly.com.

Editor: Brian Sawyer

Production Editor: Kristen Borg

Proofreader: Kristen Borg

Indexer: Sarah Milstein

Design: Monica Kamsvaag, Suzy Wivott, Ron Bilodeau, and Edie Freedman

Printing History:
First Edition: June 2009
Second Edition: November 2011

ISBN: 9781449314200

[TI]

[11/11]

ABOUT THE AUTHORS

Tim O'Reilly (@timoreilly)

Tim O'Reilly is the founder and CEO of O'Reilly Media, Inc., thought by many to be the best computer book publisher in the world. O'Reilly Media also hosts conferences on technology topics, including the O'Reilly Open Source Convention, the Web 2.0 Summit, Strata: The Business of Data, and many others. O'Reilly's *Make:* magazine and Maker Faire have been compared to the West Coast Computer Faire, which launched the personal computer revolution. Tim's company blog, O'Reilly Radar, "watches the alpha geeks" to determine emerging technology trends, and serves as a platform for advocacy about issues of importance to the technical community. Tim is also a partner at O'Reilly AlphaTech Ventures, O'Reilly's early stage venture firm, and is on the board of Safari Books Online. More at *http://radar.oreilly.com*.

Sarah Milstein (@SarahM)

Sarah Milstein, a frequent speaker on Twitter for business, has been UBM TechWeb's General Manager and co-chair for Web 2.0 Expo, an influential conference on entrepreneurship and technology. Previously, she was on the senior editorial staff at O'Reilly Media, where she founded the Tools of Change for Publishing (TOC) conference and led development of the Missing Manuals, a best-selling series of computer books for non-geeks. Before joining O'Reilly, Sarah was a freelance writer and editor, and a regular contributor to the *New York Times*. She was also the CSA program founder for Just Food, a local-food-and-farms non-profit, and co-founder of Two Tomatoes Records, a label that distributes and promotes the work of children's musician Laurie Berkner. She holds an M.B.A. from U.C. Berkeley. Bonus fact: she was the 21st user of Twitter. More at *http://sarahmilstein.com*.

CONTENTS

Introduction 5

1. Get Started 19

Sign up 21

Understand what "following" means 23

Don't follow people yet 25

Quickly create a compelling profile 27

Find the people you know on Twitter 29

Get suggestions for cool people to follow 31

Tweet from the road 33

Test-drive the 140-character limit 35

Trim messages that are too long 37

The secret to linking in Twitter 39

Figure out how many people to follow 41

Join a conversation: the hashtag (#) demystified 43

Key Twitter jargon: tweet 45

Key Twitter jargon: @messages 47

Key Twitter jargon: retweet 49

Key Twitter jargon: DM 51

Key Twitter jargon: trending topics 53

Key Twitter jargon: tweetup 55

Twitter jargon: Fail Whale 57

Try it for three weeks or your money back—guaranteed! 59

Get help from Twitter 61

2. Listen In 63

Use Twitter search 65

Take advantage of advanced search 67

Four important things to search for 69

Save searches 71

Track search with email alerts 73

Hunt down—and back up—older tweets 75

Search the nooks, crannies and archives of your account 77

Stay on top of several searches at once, including live-event coverage 79

Track tweeted links to your website 81

Dig deeper on trending topics 83

Find out what people are reading 85

Bookmark links for later reading and draw attention to tweets now 87

Use a life-changing third-party program   89
Life-changing program #1: Seesmic   91
Life-changing program #2: TweetDeck   93
Use a great mobile client   95
Follow smart people you don't know   97
Figure out who's influential on Twitter   99
Keep track of friends and family   101

3. Hold Great Conversations 103
Get great followers   105
Reply to your @messages   107
Retweet clearly and classily:
  Part 1—the overview   109
Retweet clearly and classily:
  Part 2—retweets vs. quoted tweets   111
Retweet clearly and classily:
  Part 3—use the Retweet button   113
Retweet clearly and classily:
  Part 4—quote a tweet   115

What to retweet   117
Troubleshoot your retweets   119
Ask questions   121
Answer questions   123
Send smart @replies   125
Get attention gracefully   127
Twitter often...but not too often   129
Three cool hashtag tricks   131
Know your followers   133
Unfollow graciously   135
Don't auto-DM (for crying out loud)   137
Don't spam anyone   139
Don't let third-party apps spam (or tweet)
  on your behalf   141
Fight spam   143
Recover fast if your account is
  compromised   145

4. Share Information and Ideas . . 147
Be interesting to other people 149
Make sure your messages get seen 151
Link to interesting stuff around the Web 153
Link appealingly to your blog or site 155
Use the hub-and-spoke model
  to your advantage 157
Link to a tweet 159
Post pictures 161
Live-tweet an event 163
Provide customer feedback—griping
  and glowing 165
Overhear things 167
Publish on Twitter 169
Participate in fundraising campaigns 171
Make smart suggestions on
  FollowFriday 173
Mark tweets as favorites to draw
  attention to them 175
Post on the right days and at
  the right times 177
Repost important tweets 179

5. Reveal Yourself 181
Post personal updates 183
Go beyond "What's happening?" 185
Use the right icon 187
Fill out your full bio
  (it takes two seconds) 189
Spiff up your background 191
Cross-post to Facebook, LinkedIn,
  and more 193
Divulge your location 195
Post your Twitter handle widely 197

**6. Twitter for Business: Special
   Considerations and Ideas** 199
Listen first 201
Have clear goals 203
Integrate with your other channels 205
Start slow, then build 207
Figure out who does the tweeting 209
Reveal the person behind the curtain 211
Manage multiple staffers on one account 213

Coordinate multiple accounts   215

Be conversational   217

Retweet your customers   219

Offer solid customer support   221

Post mostly NOT about your company   223

Link creatively to your own sites   225

Make money with Twitter   227

Advertise on Twitter...maybe   229

Report problems...and resolutions   231

Post personal updates   233

Use Bit.ly to track click-throughs and
    create custom short domains and URLs   235

Engage journalists and PR people   237

Follow everyone who follows you
    (almost)   239

Four services for measuring Twitter   241

Three bonus tools for business accounts   242

**Continuing the conversation—
and taking a break from it** 244

Index 245

ix

#TwitterBook

The hashtag for this book is #TwitterBook

Hashtag? **Whaaat?**

A hashtag is a term, prefixed by the # symbol, that helps people categorize messages in Twitter. In Chapters 1 and 3, we explain how they work and how you can use them in a bunch of cool ways.

If you're already comfortable with hashtags, we encourage you to use this one if you want to tweet about the book. We'll be excited to see messages about how the book has helped you, and we'll try to answer questions you may have.

Introduction

In March 2006, a little communications service called Twttr debuted. It began as a side project at a San Francisco podcasting company, but it wasn't long before the side project had become the main event.

Today, just over five years later, Twitter is booming. In September 2011, the service announced that it had 100 million active monthly users, 400 million monthly visits to its website (up from 250 million in January 2011), and served billions of messages a week around the globe. In addition, the site is now available in 17 languages (and people tweet in more languages than that).

Twitter has become a key communications channel during major political events and natural disasters. And businesses now rely on it for marketing, PR and customer service.

This book will help you understand why Twitter has become a powerhouse—the ways **it's useful and addictive and unlike any other communications service—and how you can tap that power.**

twitter

To all twitterers , if u c me n public come say hi, we r not the same we r from twitteronia, we connect

3:37 PM Feb 19th from txt

THE_REAL_SHAQ

What is Twitter?

Twitter is a messaging service that shares a lot of characteristics with communication tools you already use. It has elements that are similar to email, IM, texting, blogging, RSS and so on. But a few factors, particularly in combination, make Twitter unique:

Messages you send and receive on Twitter are no more than 140 characters, or about the length of a news headline. That means they're **really easy to write and read.**

Messages on Twitter are public, like blog posts, and you don't have to give people permission to see what you've written. That means **you can readily meet new people on Twitter.**

The messages are opt-in, and people choose to get a stream of others' messages. (On Twitter, this model is called "following," covered in Chapter 1). That means **you have to be interesting,** or people will choose not to get your updates.

You can send and receive the messages via a variety of mechanisms, including mobile phones, PCs, websites and desktop programs, and they're distributed instantaneously (or, if you prefer jargon: *in real time*). That means that Twitter can **fit with nearly anyone's workflow.**

When you add all that together, and you throw in a dose of the friendliness common on Twitter, you get a powerful and appealing communications platform that turns out to be highly useful for a slew of personal and professional needs. Shaquille O'Neal (@THE_REAL_SHAQ) sums it up here.

I don't know about you, but I always get all teary-eyed watching space launches. Deeply touched by fellow humans, able to do this.

3:56 PM Mar 15th from web

jamesoreilly
James O'Reilly

Our exterminator guy is handsome, smart, sweet, experienced, inexpensive. Couldn't make him up.

12:44 PM Mar 27th from web

jamesoreilly
James O'Reilly

 @kati
Kati

Locked myself out of my room and my roommate sleeps in ear plugs. This should be interesting...

23 Mar via Twitter for iPhone   ☆ Favorite   ⇄ Retweet   ↩ Reply

 @kati
Kati

It's weird how when you go off to college, life at home goes on without you. #growingup

19 Sep via txt   ☆ Favorite   ⇄ Retweet   ↩ Reply

What's Twitter good for?
Ambient intimacy

Twitter poses the question, "What's happening?" Sometimes, people answer pretty dutifully. So they're eating bacon for lunch, catching up on email run amok or cleaning the tub. Because they can send updates not only from their computers but from their mobile phones, too, people also report that they're ordering a triple double at In-N-Out Burger, sitting in traffic on Route 1 or boarding a plane for Omaha.

Although status updates like that may sound mundane, people on Twitter have found that becoming aware of what your friends, family and colleagues are doing (without having to respond) leads to a **lightweight but meaningful connection,** sometimes called "ambient awareness" or "ambient intimacy," a term coined by Leisa Reichelt (@leisa).

Tim on ambient intimacy: I see my brother James every couple of months, talk to him about as often, always wish for more. Through Twitter, I follow him every day. Of course, we have shared context that others may miss. Naturally, he tears up at a space launch: when we were kids we used to pray each night for a UFO to come down in our backyard. And it's great to know that he's got an exterminator in to deal with the biting spiders that kept me from staying over last time I visited. I know, as few do, that his background is a photo from my father's grave in Ireland.

Sarah on ambient intimacy: My partner's younger sister, Kati, is in college. Though these snapshots may seem random, they help me understand her day-to-day life there. Even better, when we talk, instead of having this conversation—Me: "How's it going?" K: "Good."—I'll ask how she got back into her room and get a funny story, or I'll ask what felt weird to miss, and we'll get into a deeper discussion we otherwise wouldn't have had.

@JamilSmith
Jamil Smith

Seven-year-old girl critiques @DCComics for sexualizing one of her heroines in their reboot. My Lord, does she get it. goo.gl/DXU4J

27 Sep via TweetDeck ☆ Favorite ⇄ Retweet ↰ Reply

@jimog
Jim O'Grady

Proud of this. Give it a listen, won't you? Comedy Since 9/11: Comics Reflect On What It Took To Get NY Laughing Again. bit.ly/o86JYf

5 Sep via web ☆ Favorite ⇄ Retweet ↰ Reply

@tonystubblebine
Tony Stubblebine

Powerful photo from the the White House Situation Room yesterday. Gives the impression that senior leaders are human. http://bit.ly/lA2PVS

2 May via web ☆ Favorite ⇄ Retweet ↰ Reply
from New York, NY

@xenijardin
Xeni Jardin

Meanwhile in NYC: this video shows a young woman, peaceful protestor, being maced in the face by police. boingboing.net/2011/09/25/vid...

25 Sep via Twitter for Mac ☆ Favorite ⇄ Retweet ↰ Reply

What's Twitter good for?
Sharing media and commentary

Although Twitter started out as a service for people to post personal updates, it's become a critical channel for sharing media. People use it to talk about—and link to—the things they're reading, watching, listening to and thinking about. Indeed, many people use it primarily for sharing or finding links to stuff that interests them. Twitter has thus become a key player in the attention economy, helping people **disseminate media and ideas they care about.**

As part of the Internet, Twitter is, naturally, home to a lot of commentary, too. It's the site of debates about topical issues, editorializing on links that people distribute and protests about media, corporate behavior and government.

As you'll see later in the book, Twitter is also good for sharing humor, expertise, appeals for help and much more.

@veen
Jeffrey Veen

Our immediate response to the earthquake? Get in a doorway? Get under the desk? Nope. "Check Twitter!"

30 Mar 09 via web ☆ Favorite ⇄ Retweet ↰ Reply

 @yasminerashidi
Yasmine El Rashidi

Heading to #tahrir with others -- bringing medical supplies. Anything needed urgently let us know #egypt

28 Jun via Twitter for BlackBerry® ☆ Favorite ⇄ Retweet ↰ Reply

 @kimseverson
Kim Severson ✔

Protestors quiet. Police quiet. #TroyDavis family quiet. Heat, wait and emotional exhaustion taking its toll.

21 Sep via Twitter for iPhone ☆ Favorite ⇄ Retweet ↰ Reply

 @jkrums
Janis Krums

http://twitpic.com/135xa - There's a plane in the Hudson. I'm on the ferry going to pick up the people. Crazy.

What's Twitter good for?
Breaking news and shared experiences

Several times a year, there's a big event—be it terrorist attacks in Mumbai, elections in Iran, revolution in Cairo or earthquake in New York City—where people say, "Wow, **Twitter really changed the way that unfolded.** This is the first time it's been a major channel for breaking news." And as the number of people on Twitter grows, there's always somebody having that experience anew. But the truth is, Twitter has been the world's real-time newspaper since at least July 2008, when people realized that tweets about the Los Angeles earthquake that month preceded mainstream media reports by as much as ten minutes.

Then, in January 2009, within minutes of a US Airways plane's landing in the Hudson River, Janis Krums (@jkrums), a nearby ferry passenger, tweeted a picture and comment that were widely distributed via Twitter that day—and which scooped the news media on a story happening in their own backyard. Since then, Twitter has evolved into the go-to service for news from people on the ground during major happenings around the globe. Nowadays, it's also used by professional journalists who augment their regular reporting with more-immediate tweets. In the bottom example here, in September 2011, *New York Times* reporter Kim Severson (@kimseverson) observed the scene outside the prison where people waited to hear whether the Supreme Court would stay Troy Davis's execution.

The service has thus become **a great tool for sharing common experiences.** Those include not only emergencies, like natural disasters and terrorist attacks, but also organized events, like conferences and concerts. While a surge of messages on Twitter can break news, the individual posts help people verify what's happening, connect with resources, and, during emergencies, let others know whether they're safe.

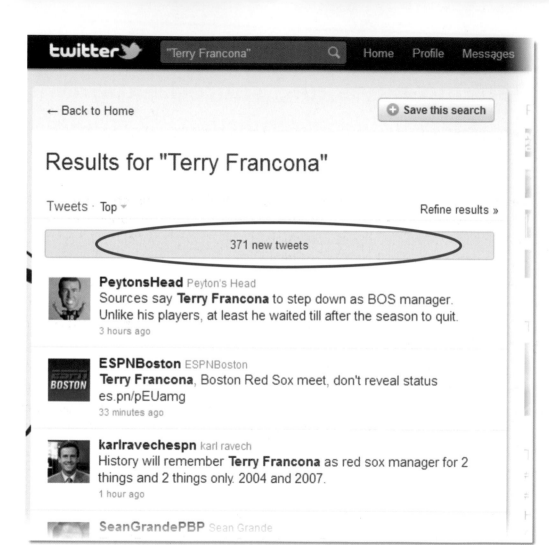

What's Twitter good for?
Mind reading—and mind opening

Whether you have an account on Twitter or not, the site's search service is **an amazing mind-reading tool, letting you see not just what individuals are thinking about, but what groups are focusing on, too.**

A well-honed search can reveal how other people feel about your company, your latest public talk and your favorite TV show. The ten trending topics that appear on the search page and change constantly give you insight into the things a lot of people find important at any given moment (we talk more about trends in Chapter 2).

Key to this element of Twitter is that the search results update in *real time.* Here, you can see results for a search about Terry Francona, the Boston Red Sox manager, on a morning rumors were swirling about his leaving the team. From the initial search, it took about 10 minutes for the 371 new tweets to accumulate.

More subtly, mind-reading on Twitter can increase your compassion. When you follow a number of people of another race, religion or political persuasion, to name a few groups, you can gain valuable perspective on how people who are different from you experience the world—particularly if they're under-represented in the mainstream media. Often, you'll see surprising patterns emerge, making it a powerful way to open your own mind.

@CoryBooker
Cory Booker ✓

I'm getting reports on that. I'll try 2 help
RT @ConceitedGansta: @Newark4311
Power out. Is there an outage in the area
of nye ave & schley

6 Sep via UberSocial for BlackBerry ☆ Unfavorite ⇄ Retweet ↩ Reply

@CoryBooker
Cory Booker ✓

Visiting police at 2nd Precinct & yes... I'm
bringing pizza. Mild Mannered Mayor by
day & Prodigious Pizza Pusher in weather
emergencies

28 Aug via Twitter for BlackBerry® ☆ Unfavorite ⇄ Retweet ↩ Reply

@CoryBooker
Cory Booker ✓

Send me a DM, let's talk RT
@JanetChess: My company, Xerox, would
like to help #MakeADifference in Newark.
How can we help?

4 Sep via UberSocial for BlackBerry ☆ Un...

@CoryBooker
Cory Booker ✓

I'm walking in Central Ward sharing job
information and taking community
concerns. Right now on Irving Turner
Blvd.

24 Sep via UberSocial for BlackBerry ☆

@CoryBooker
Cory Booker ✓

So so awesome! RT @NmJean05: In light
of #9/11 I am volunteering cleaning up a
school over in North Newark, on
Saturday.

9 Sep via UberSocial for BlackBerry ☆ Unfavorite ⇄ Retweet ↩ Reply

What's Twitter good for?
Business and civic conversations

Twitter has emerged as **a key business channel,** letting companies engage with customers, partners and other constituents in a direct way that's both personal and public—something no other medium allows. Businesses are monitoring what people think of their products, responding to customer service requests, having conversations with stakeholders and making money through creative promotions of various kinds. (Chapter 6 covers it all.)

Celebrities and politicians, themselves mini-businesses, are engaging with their fans and constituents in new ways. Consider Cory Booker, the mayor of Newark, NJ, and a prolific and innovative user of Twitter. He manages to inspire, lead, respond and reveal himself through his tweets, often simultaneously.

We show a few representative examples here. The top two are just a sliver of the tweeting Booker did during Hurricane Irene, and they reflect his activity during weather emergencies generally: he spends a lot of time moving around his city, publicly responding to residents' concerns and sharing his frankly corny sense of humor when people need levity. In the third example, he responds—again publicly—to a major business that wants to work in Newark, instilling a sense of pride. In the fourth example, he simply tells people that he's out in a neighborhood where they can find him and talk. In the fifth, he retweets a resident who's volunteering for the city, shining a light on their efforts and giving others a sense of the good that happens in Newark. We ran out of room, or we would've also included Booker's inspirational quotes, his tweets about his own diet and exercise attempts, and his retweets of residents' shout-outs about *their* dieting and exercising along with him. Read on to learn not only how to follow him, but also how to create such a terrific Twitter presence yourself.

CHAPTER 1 | Get Started

Twitter lives a dual life. On the one hand, it's a simple service. Besides letting you share and read very short messages, it has few bells and whistles. On the other hand, it can be surprisingly hard to figure out. The screens aren't particularly intuitive, and the jargon and symbols are obscure. Even more vexing, it's not clear at first why people are so enthusiastic about Twitter. **What makes it fun? Useful? Revolutionary?**

In the Introduction, we showed you a few great uses for Twitter. In this chapter, we help you get set up and explain some key ways to communicate successfully on the service. We also decode the most common jargon and symbols. (By the way, if you need a version of Twitter that works with assistive technologies, try **EasyChirp** [http://easychirp.com]; it's also good for low-vision users, keyboard-only users, and—if you're still living in 1932—Internet Explorer 6 users.)

Of course, listening to others is one of the things Twitter is best for—and you don't need an account to do it. If you're all about tuning into the buzz, skip ahead to Chapter 2.

Amanda Jones

✓ Name looks great.

amanda.jones@email.com

✓ We will email you a confirmation.

•••••••••

✗ Password is too obvious.

AmandaJones91

✓ Username is available.

Suggestions: Jones91Jones · JonesJones91 · Jones91Amanda

☑ Keep me logged-in on this computer.

By clicking the button, you agree to the terms below:

These Terms of Service ("**Terms**") govern your access to and use of the services and Twitter's websites (the "**Services**"), and any information, text, graphics, photos or other materials

Printable versions:
Terms of Service · Privacy Policy

Create my account

Note: Others will be able to find you by name, username or email. Your email will not be shown publicly. You can change your privacy settings at any time.

Sign up

Signing up takes just a few minutes. Head to **Twitter** (http://twitter.com) and under "New to Twitter? Join today!", fill in your actual name (or company name, if this is a corporate account), email address and password.

The next screen you see looks like the one here. The Username box is where you add your account name—the one everybody on Twitter will know you by, like THE_REAL_SHAQ or Pistachio or timoreilly (the @ symbol has a special role in usernames, explained later in this chapter). Twitter suggests usernames based on your actual name, but you can change it, and it automatically tells you if the one you've typed in is available. **For the username, try to find one with the fewest number of characters possible;** that becomes important as soon as people want to refer to you or repost your comments and find that your username is taking up a slew of their 140 characters. (You can change the username later, but it's really the key piece of your identity on Twitter, so be thoughtful in your choice.)

After you've made any adjustments, click "Create my account." Twitter now walks you through a few steps to find your friends on the service and suggest other people you might want to follow (explained later in this chapter). Before you charge through the steps to find and follow people, we recommend that you read page 27 and flesh out your account so that other people find it appealing.

Kat Meyer

@KatMeyer Tucson

Champion of storytelling in all forms + formats. Co-Chair:
O'Reilly's TOC; Co-hostess: #followreader; Heart biggest:
http://www.t
http://about.me/

About @KatMeyer

26,308	4,948	8,338	663
Tweets	Following	Followers	Listed

hair:
gest:

About @KatMeyer

26,308	4,948	8,338	663
Tweets	Following	Followers	Listed

Understand what "following" means

With the exception of accounts that have been protected, messages on Twitter are public. Like blog posts, anyone can see them. But the way nearly everyone sees other people's messages is by choosing to get a stream of the updates from people they're interested in. On Twitter, this opt-in model is called *following*. Here you can see that more than 8,300 people have chosen to follow Kat Meyer (@KatMeyer).

When you follow somebody, you receive a message every time he updates. When somebody follows you, he receives your message every time you update. Unlike a lot of social software, however, following on Twitter is what geeks call *asymmetric*. That is, **you don't have to agree to follow each other in order to see somebody's messages.**

There are two key implications of this model:

1. Because you don't have to verify each other, you're much more likely on Twitter than other social networks to find people you don't already know. That makes the site good for professional networking.

2. If you aren't interesting, people will unfollow you, or they'll never follow you in the first place. The opt-in arrangement means that Twitter rewards interestingness. Use your 140 characters wisely.

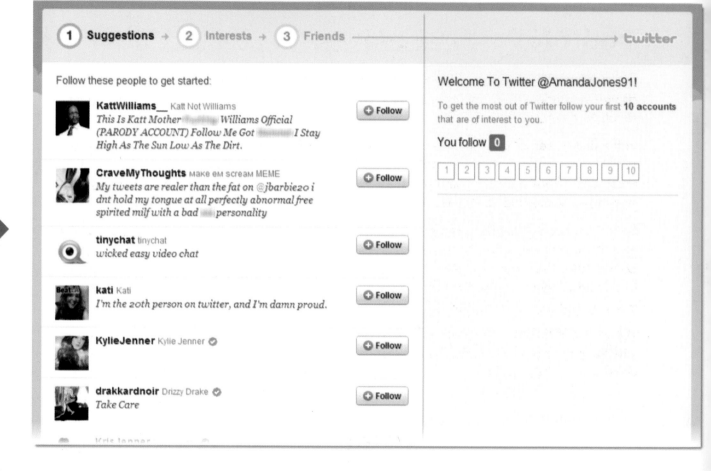

① **Suggestions** → ② Interests → ③ Friends ───────────→ twitter

Follow these people to get started:

KattWilliams__ Katt Not Williams
*This Is Katt Mother ▓▓▓▓ Williams Official
(PARODY ACCOUNT) Follow Me Got ▓▓▓▓ I Stay
High As The Sun Low As The Dirt.*

⊕ Follow

CraveMyThoughts мαке ем scream MEME
*My tweets are realer than the fat on @jbarbie2o i
dnt hold my tongue at all perfectly abnormal free
spirited milf with a bad ▓▓ personality*

⊕ Follow

tinychat tinychat
wicked easy video chat

⊕ Follow

kati Kati
I'm the 2oth person on twitter, and I'm damn proud.

⊕ Follow

KylieJenner Kylie Jenner ✔
⊕ Follow

drakkardnoir Drizzy Drake ✔
Take Care

⊕ Follow

Kris Jenner

Welcome To Twitter @AmandaJones91!

To get the most out of Twitter follow your first **10 accounts**
that are of interest to you.

You follow **0**

| 1 | 2 | 3 | 4 | 5 | 6 | 7 | 8 | 9 | 10 |

Don't follow people yet

For most people, Twitter makes sense only when you're following other people. So as soon as you've created an account, but before you've filled out your profile, Twitter prompts you to follow others.

In the first screen of suggestions, shown here, Twitter lists a bunch of random accounts you might want to follow. **But there's no reason to follow random strangers. So skip this step** (there's a Skip button at the bottom of the page), and instead move to the next few steps, where you can choose accounts based on interests and people you know.

Better yet, skip all the steps that direct you to follow people now and move right along to the end of the process, where you can fill out your profile. Why? Because when you follow other people, they usually get a notice that you've done so, and they may check out your account to decide whether they want to follow you back. If your profile is blank, they're unlikely to follow you (blank profiles look a lot like spammers).

The next page gives you tips on creating a follow-friendly profile. Once you've done that, you can get back to the features that help you find people to follow, covered later in this chapter.

David Pogue ✔

@Pogue USA

Tech columnist, NY Times; CNBC tech dude; Missing Manuals creator, dad of 3!

http://davidpogue.com/

Chris Brogan ✔

@chrisbrogan Boston, MA

President, Human Business Works. More? http://bit.ly /cbbio . contact: http://chrisbrogan.com/contact

http://chrisbrogan.com

Chris Atherton

@finiteattention Manchester/London/wherever.

UX specialist, info-architect and behavioural scientist. I want to help you understand your users and improve your product's awesomeness. Hire me? I'm lovely.

http://about.me/cjatherton

Quickly create a compelling profile

As soon as you create an account on Twitter, people can—and often will—start checking out your page, particularly if you follow them first. So **before you start clicking around, spend three minutes setting up your profile.**

On the upper-right corner of your account page, click the arrow next your username, and then Settings. The page you hit next has tabs across the top. On the Account tab, make sure to turn on the last setting, "Always use HTTPS", which improves your security. You can also adjust a bunch of features, including the option to add a general location to your tweets (more on that in Chapter 5). Finally, if you want to keep your messages private, click "Protect my tweets." (Nearly everyone leaves them public.) When you're done, click Save.

Now pop over to the Profile tab. Nothing says, "I'm a newbie and maybe a spammer" like the default icon, so upload a photo, drawing or logo. Next fill in your location. Unlike the location option on the Account tab, this one is static—it's simply whatever you type in—and it's worth adding because it gives you credibility. Now add a URL that helps people learn more about you. It can be your blog, website, LinkedIn profile, etcetera.

Finally, the fun part: the Bio box, which gives you just 160 characters to tell your life story. We show three good examples here. One common approach is to list a series of words or phrases, like David Pogue (@Pogue). Chris Brogan (@chrisbrogan) is smart in giving you more ways to contact him. Some craft a story, like Chris Atherton (@finiteattention), who uses the bio in an ingenious way. After you've crafted your masterpiece, click Save.

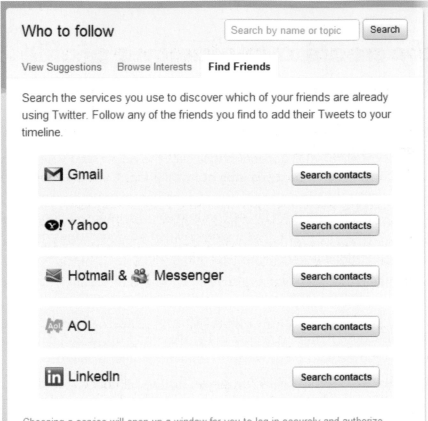

Who to follow

Search by name or topic   Search

View Suggestions   Browse Interests   **Find Friends**

Search the services you use to discover which of your friends are already using Twitter. Follow any of the friends you find to add their Tweets to your timeline.

Gmail   Search contacts

Yahoo   Search contacts

Hotmail & Messenger   Search contacts

AOL   Search contacts

LinkedIn   Search contacts

Choosing a service will open up a window for you to log in securely and authorize Twitter to see your contacts. You'll only see users who have allowed their accounts to be found by email address. **Don't worry:** we won't share your contacts with anybody or email anyone without your consent.

Find the people you know on Twitter

Twitter gives you a couple of tools to **discover people you already know who are tweeting.** At the top of your Twitter account page, click "Who To Follow" → "Find Friends" to get the page shown here (if your account is brand-new, you may also see a link on the right side of the page "Look for your friends").

If you want to find a particular person or company on Twitter, use the search box at the top.

If you want to find people you know who are already on Twitter, use the "Search contacts" options for your various other accounts. (These options work differently for each type of account, but all are fairly clear and none will mistakenly spam your whole address book.) This feature is especially handy, because a lot of people sign up for Twitter using their regular email address but a variation of their name you might not think to search for.

twitter tip

When you follow somebody on Twitter, he gets an email notification. Not to encourage stalking, but if you follow a person via a list, he'll never know you're following him—or if you've unfollowed him. Chapter 2 describes lists in juicy detail.

What's happening?

Timeline   @Mentions   Retweets ▾   Searches ▾   Lists ▾

susanorlean Susan Orlean
I love when people start emails to me "Dear Susan". So civil! Such a
nice change from "Hey" or just diving in. #oldschool
2 minutes ago

thenation The Nation
Steve Earle & Allison Moorer special musical guests on 14th annual
@thenation Cruise! "The Love Boat for Policy Wonks". bit.ly/bbdNGv
3 minutes ago

hannahmw23 Hannah Wallace
Bittman linked to my Q&A With Debra Eschmeyer in his blog about
Food Corps!: nyti.ms/qPXHnR
5 minutes ago

AAUW AAUW
RT @msmagazine: mRT @d_doucet An interesting Infographic
about number of women writers in the 2010-11 primetime season
goo.gl/pq7h5
5 minutes ago

bellhistory W. Bell ⟲ by thenation
Thinking about getting a PhD? Read this. Faulty Towers: The Crisis

Get suggestions for cool people to follow

While Twitter is great for staying connected to people you already know, it's **at least as good for meeting and hearing from people you don't yet know.** Here's any easy way to get suggestions for people to follow.

At the top of your home page, click "Who To Follow" → "Browse Interests" to reach a page where Twitter has categorized a bunch of compelling accounts. Once you follow a few, your home page looks like this, with incoming tweets from people you're now following.

For more suggested people to follow, we *cannot* recommend the tab labeled "View Suggestions". The accounts on that tab appear to be random, at best. So while it can't hurt to take a look, it's probably not your best use of time. Instead, if you're seeking more people to follow, check out lists, described in Chapter 2.

twitter tip

Simply clicking around is a decent way to find accounts to follow. See who the people you now follow are following, and check out the accounts that are getting retweeted a lot (we explain retweets in Chapter 3).

Turning Mobile Twitter Updates Off and On

- **ON:** turns ALL your authorized Twitter updates and notifications on.

- **OFF:** turns off all updates except direct messages. Send STOP again to turn off direct messages too.

- **STOP, QUIT, End, Cancel, Arret** or **Unsubscribe**: turns ALL phone notifications off.
- **ON username**: turns on notifications for a specific person on your phone. Example: **ON** alissa
- **OFF username**: turns off notifications for a specific person on your phone. Example: **OFF** blaine
- **FOLLOW username:** this command allows you to start following a specific user, as well as receive SMS notifications. Example: **FOLLOW** jerry, or **f** jerry for short.
- **LEAVE username:** this command allows you to stop receiving SMS notifications for a specific user. Example: **LEAVE** benfu, or **l** benfu for short.

Tweet from the road

Part of Twitter's beauty is that you can send and receive messages from your desktop *and* from your mobile phone—meaning Twitter goes where you go. Many people find that because their status changes a lot when they're out and about, mobile **updates on the phone are a natural fit.**

If have a smartphone, you can skip the SMS geekery here by using one of the sleek mobile Twitter clients described in Chapter 2. Not only are they easier and more fun, they also save you SMS charges. (That said, if you want Twitter available for use during emergencies, it's a good idea to set up the SMS service, which your mobile carrier is more likely to keep running even if other data services go down.)

For the SMS service, first set your account to send and receive tweets via text message. On your home page, find your account name in the upper-right corner, click the arrow, and then Settings → Mobile. Type in your phone number, and then click Start to initiate a verification process that Twitter walks you through. Your mobile carrier will charge you standard text-messaging rates for Twitter updates, so keep an eye on volume. (As we describe in Chapter 2, you can specify which of your followees' messages you get via text.)

To post a message from your phone in the US, use the code 40404. For a list of international codes, head to http://bit.ly/twt-scs.

To help make your phone use more efficient, Twitter has created a handful of commands you can use. Those shown here are from the Twitter help pages. For more tips on texting with Twitter, head to http://support.twitter.com → Apps, SMS, and Mobile → Twitter via SMS.

This unusually helpful sentence, including all of the spaces and all of the punctuation, is precisely one hundred and forty characters long.

Test-drive the 140-character limit

Twitter famously allows for messages of only 140 characters, which is about the length of a headline. To get a sense for what that feels like, type up a message in the "What's happening?" box. As you type, the Twitter website counts down your remaining characters (look just below the box where you're typing). If you're texting on a phone, remember to use just 140 of the 160 characters in your outgoing messages.

As you can see here, **140 characters is approximately a sentence, maybe two.** Bear in mind that your 140 characters includes spaces.

By the way, posts on Twitter are capped at 140 characters for a reason: text messages on your phone are limited to just 160 characters. Twitter takes that base and reserves 20 characters for usernames, leaving you with a tidy 140.

twitter tip

Wondering what to tweet about? In the Introduction and throughout the rest of the book, we offer ideas and examples of great things to post. Or look on Twitter, find somebody whose messages you like, and then mimic his style and get inspiration from his topics.

@xenijardin
Xeni Jardin

Bout half my family&friends in VA are w/o power. All safe. Some fallen trees, 2 of which smashed some of my mom's windows, blocking her car.

27 Aug via Twitter for iPhone ☆ Favorite ⇄ Retweet

@SarahM
Sarah Milstein

V nice MT @tarasophia: On what Top 5 list would I possibly be right after David Brooks & right b4 James Frey? This one! bit.ly/rnpMTY

21 Sep via web ☆ Favorite ↩ Reply ☰ Delete

@jenbee
Jen Bekman

Passed Cooper's freshman class loading in @ St Mark's dorm + childless tho I may be, felt more kinship w/ the parents.
#42lessthanaweekaway

Trim messages that are too long

If your message bulges above 140 characters, **here are a few common tricks you can use to tighten them up** (we discuss URL shorteners later in this chapter):

1. Use a plus sign (+) or ampersand (&) instead of "and."

2. Leave out periods and other punctuation, especially at the end of a sentence.

3. Use common and not-so-common abbreviations where the meaning is clear.

4. Omit "I" and perhaps the verb "to be."

5. Use numerals instead of writing out the numbers.

6. Lotta times, you can cut the first few words of a sentence or even space between words.

twitter tip

If you need help shrinking your prose down to 140 characters, try **140it** (http://140it.com), which uses common cutting conventions to whittle down potential posts. Some of the third-party clients described in Chapter 2 will also help you trim tweets.

The secret to linking in Twitter

The instant you want to post a link on Twitter, you realize that **most URLs don't come close to fitting in your 140-character limit—especially if you've actually said anything in the message.** The good news is that you can get help from URL shorteners, services that take a URL and shrink it down to somewhere between 10 and 30 characters.

If you post a link from the Twitter website, Twitter itself automatically shortens your link, using 20 characters (when you paste in your URL, the counter below the "What's happening" box takes those 20 characters into account). On the Twitter site, the shortened link will appear as a cut-off version of the original URL, something like nytimes.com/top/features...; on other sites, it will appear as a t.co link, something like http://t.co/xyz. In fact, all of the major Twitter clients (described in Chapter 2) have built-in link-shorteners.

If you want more sophisticated shortening features, try **Bit.ly** (http://bit.ly), shown here. It lets you customize short URLs and track click-throughs, among other tricks. (In Chapter 6, we talk more about the service.)

Incidentally, you may have heard that shortened links aren't safe to click because they hide the destination URL. While it's never a good idea to click links from people you don't know who are promising amazing diet results, research has shown that 99.94% of short URLs are safe (that's better odds than Google results). This link—we promise it's not concealing porn—takes you to a link-safety report by the research team from Zscaler (@zscaler), a cloud-computing security firm: http://bit.ly/zscaler-safe.

brady forrest

@brady seattle, WA USA

Ignite, O'Reilly Radar, Where 2.0, Web 2.0 Expo
http://radar.oreilly.com/brady

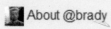 About @brady

3,402	**2,028**	**9,428**	**648**
Tweets	Following	Followers	Listed

Tim O'Reilly ✔

@timoreilly Sebastopol, CA

Founder and CEO, O'Reilly Media. Watching the alpha geeks, sharing their stories, helping the future unfold.
http://radar.oreilly.com

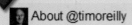 About @timoreilly

15,813	**755**	**1,490,211**	**19,816**
Tweets	Following	Followers	Listed

Sarah Milstein

@SarahM Bklyn + SF

Co-chair of Web2Expo + co-author of
http://bit.ly/TheTwitterBook. Also: a fan of vegetables,
dogs, shoes. sarah.milstein@gmail.com
http://sarahmilstein.com

About @SarahM

9,772	**361**	**11,909**	**475**
Tweets	Following	Followers	Listed

Rec___ ___ages

Figure out how many people to follow

Everyone has a different theory of how many people you should follow. Some say 50 is the optimal number. Others argue that 100 is perfect. A lot of people follow 500 or 5,000. Many believe you should follow everybody who follows you—though we're of the strong opinion that part of the beauty of Twitter is that you don't need to follow everyone mutually. Indeed, while your mother may be offended if you don't follow her, following a lot of people you don't find interesting is a sure way to make Twitter useless to you.

Given the range of opinions, **you should feel confident in doing whatever works best for you.** To figure that out, try following 40 or 100 people for a few weeks, and see how that works. Follow more or unfollow people as you see fit (in Chapter 3, we talk about the perceived politics of unfollowing; but in a nutshell, we say don't sweat it).

If you want to filter or group your incoming messages in order to keep a closer eye on just a few followees, we give tips for that in Chapter 2.

twitter tip

Businesses on Twitter have different issues than individuals about whom to follow. In Chapter 6, we talk about corporate considerations.

@BuddyMedia
Buddy Media

Our own @joeciarallo wants to moderate a panel w/ @StarwoodBuzz, #Gansevoort & @GrandLifeHotels for #SXSW. Vote now! bddy.me/oR7sXD

35 minutes ago via HootSuite ☆ Favorite ⇄ Retweet ↩ Reply

@anildash
Anil Dash

So far the worst damage #Irene has caused is to people's common sense when retweeting questionable photos.

27 Aug via Twitter for Mac ☆ Unfavorite ⇄ Retweet ↩ Reply

@heymarci
marci alboher ✓

#FF Personal finance go-to sources (& generally fun/interesting on Twitter) @LaurenYoung @ManishaThakor

3 Jun via HootSuite ☆ Favorite ⇄ Retweet ↩ Reply

@susanorlean
Susan Orlean ✓

Moving on Friday to California. JUST REALIZED I FORGOT TO PACK. #panic #superpanic #iampanicking #doiseemcalm #iamnot #foamingatthemouth

3 hours ago via HootSuite ☆ Favorite ⇄ Retweet ↩ Reply

Join a conversation: the hashtag (#) demystified

People new to Twitter find hashtags among the most confusing aspects of the system. But it's an extremely useful convention, and it's **actually a simple idea, worth getting your head around.**

Because there's no way on Twitter to categorize a message or to say, "All these messages are about the same thing," users created an ad hoc solution: When somebody wants to designate related messages, they come up with a short term and prefix it with the # symbol. (In programmer-speak, that symbol is a hash mark, and the term is a tag; thus "hashtag.") Then others add the hashtag to messages about that topic—and then anyone can search that hashtag and find all the related messages.

As you can see here, hashtags serve many purposes. One common use is denoting events; #SXSW is the hashtag for the annual South by Southwest festival; #Irene is the hurricane that hit the Eastern seaboard in August 2011. Twitter memes also show up often, like #FF, which stands for "Follow Friday," described in Chapter 4. People also use hashtags as one-off comments on their posts, as Susan Orlean does cleverly here. You may also see the #fb tag; it's part of the way you can cross-post messages to Facebook, described in Chapter 5. In Chapter 3, we offer ideas on using hashtags yourself.

To see messages categorized with a hashtag, head to **Twitter search** (http://search.twitter.com, detailed in Chapter 2) and run a query for your term. **Hashtags.org** (http://hashtags.org) also shows popular hashtags and some stats on their usage. **What the Trend** (http://whatthetrend.com, described in Chapter 2) can help you figure out what current, popular hashtags are about.

@nmsanchez
nmsanchez

Don't care what the haters say. #Gaga
rules. And I tweet this as the mom of 2
young girls.

17 hours ago via Twitter for iPad ☆ Favorite ↻ Retweet ↩ Reply

@timoreilly
Tim O'Reilly ✓

In response to my tweet about ICANN,
someone pointed me to this @kevin2kelly
piece on "the Shirky principle" - how true
http://bit.ly/inwreD

26 Jun via Seesmic Desktop ☆ Favorite ↻ Retweet ↩ Reply

Key Twitter jargon: tweet

A lot of Twitter conventions and jargon—perhaps most—have **come from users rather than from the company.** The language around the service is no exception, and "tweet" is a perfect example.

A term created by users, *tweet* as a noun refers to a single Twitter post. The term is also used as a verb, as in, "We're live-tweeting the four-hour wait at Pizzeria Bianco."

Twitter calls a stream of incoming tweets a *timeline*. Thus, on your Twitter account page, look to the Timeline tab for the posts from people you follow. One mildly confusing aspect of Twitter is that when you look at your account page, you see the Timeline tab and a bunch of incoming tweets. When *other* people look at your account page, they see a Tweets tab instead, which has your outgoing messages.

twitter tip

Trivia: Twitter itself didn't incorporate the term "tweet" into its site until three years after the service started.

What's happening?

Timeline   **@Mentions**   Retweets ▾   Searches ▾   Lists ▾

Tweets mentioning @SarahM

goodappetite melissa clark
@SarahM I fixed the problem, should work now!
7 minutes ago

iamcassandra Cassandra Zink
RT @amalt Via @SarahM: Cowboy Needs a Home -- pics and info on a very adoptable Bklyn dog: bit.ly/cowboy-home. Pls RT!
18 minutes ago

amalt Anna Maltby
Via @SarahM: Cowboy Needs a Home -- pics and info on a very adoptable Bklyn dog: bit.ly/cowboy-home. Pls RT!
35 minutes ago

tamyho tam ho
In NYC looking for a dog? RT @SarahM Cowboy, the v adoptable dog staying w/me, needs a forever home: bit.ly/cowboy-home. Pls RT!
1 hour ago

cjwake Chris Wake
@SarahM congrats on the foster dog! Maybe the tread-desk is an

Key Twitter jargon: @messages

In the beginning, there was no way to send a message to anybody else on Twitter. You just used the system for posting status updates. But pretty quickly, **people found that they wanted to hold conversations on Twitter, and public conversation at that.** So users started adding the @ symbol to the beginning of account names as a way to send a public message or refer to somebody on Twitter.

After a while, Twitter itself incorporated the convention and took it a very useful step further: now, an @ symbol followed by an account name is a link to that account page. Thus @messages—also sometimes called @mentions or @replies—are a key piece of networking on Twitter, helping you discover new people.

To see @messages to you or mentioning you, head to your Twitter home page and look for the @Mentions tab. Sadly, that tab doesn't light up, and Twitter sends email notification of only some @messages, so you just have to click over occasionally to stay up to date.

twitter tip

In Chapter 3, we give tips on replying to @messages and initiating conversations. In Chapter 4, we explain why when you want everyone who follows you to see a message, you shouldn't start it with the @ symbol.

@profblmkelley
Blair LM Kelley

RT @michele_norris: Worth reading Gordy Piece about Prez Obama's CBC remarks & response in the room compared to web. wapo.st/pnyLG8

28 Sep via TweetDeck ☆ Favorite ⇄ Retweet

@petermeyers
Peter Meyers

RT @lenedgerly: This smart piece by @BradStone helps me understand how Bezos engineered today's triumph bloom.bg/r9vJq8 <-great context

@sarawinge
Sara Winge

Hint: no, and it's worse than you think! RT @bakadesuyo: Should you trust your memory? http://ht.ly/62IAQ

14 Aug via TweetDeck ☆ Favorite ⇄ Retweet ↩ Reply

Key Twitter jargon: retweet

"Retweeting" is one of the silliest-sounding terms floating around Twitter. But don't be fooled, because it's also **one of the most important.**

Retweeting is simply the act of reposting somebody else's cool or insightful or helpful tweet and giving them credit. Retweets (or RTs) help important messages work their way around Twitter. They also suggest esteem: when you RT somebody else, you implicitly say, "I respect you and your message." Indeed, as we discuss in Chapter 2, being retweeted a lot can be a sign of influence on Twitter.

In addition, as we describe on the previous page, when you use the @ symbol to refer to somebody else on Twitter—always part of a retweet—you automatically create a link to his account. Retweeting is thus part of the network system on Twitter, and it's not unlike bloggers' linking to another blog.

By the way, as you can see here, sometimes a retweet involves a comment on the original message—which is part of the fun.

In Chapter 3, we give you a bevy of tips on retweeting clearly and classily.

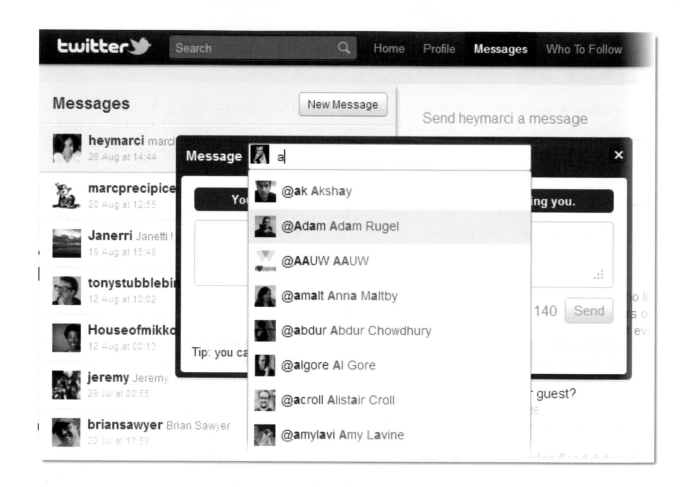

Key Twitter jargon: DM

Although messages on Twitter are public by default, **the system does have a private message option.** Private notes on Twitter are called "direct messages," or DMs, and they fit the usual 140-character mold. The tricky part is that in order for you to send a DM, the recipient has to be following you. Confusingly, if you're following somebody who isn't following you, he *can* DM you.

To see incoming DMs or send one on the Twitter website, head to the top of the page and click Messages (Twitter now officially calls DMs "messages," but everybody else calls them "DMs"). It's disturbingly easy to accidentally send a public message when you intend to DM somebody (as former NY Rep Anthony Weiner can attest), and it's even pretty easy to DM the wrong person. To cut down on mistakes, use the New Message button, which prompts you to pick a recipient from your followees. Double-check everything before hitting Send.

twitter tip

Twitter has a feature that sends an email when somebody DMs you (look under Settings → Notifications). It's a good idea to leave that on, because the Twitter site doesn't notify you in any way when you have a DM, and who wants to bother checking constantly?

Your Tweets 9,814
43 minutes ago · The New Resentment of the Poor - a w...

Following 363   Followers 11,907

View list page →

hone for my

Who to follow · refresh · view all

pattiesellers pattiesellers · Follow   ×
I'm an Editor at Large at Fortune and cochair the M...

heathr heather gold · Follow   ×
Followed by @ftrain and others.

TKColonel Tom Krackeler · Follow   ×
Followed by @chantallaurie and others.

for saying
in if they

Trends: United States · change

#ThingsWeNeedToChange

#replacebooktitleswithbacon

at this level   #WhyYoBaby
u won't know
Hello September

Goodbye August

WHY KHLEO THOMAS

ment.   George Lucas

Unstable Creatures

MSG ANNIVERSARY

The Dream

from the

Twitter · for · iPhone

Key Twitter jargon: trending topics

To make your eavesdropping easier, Twitter has a feature called Trends. It lists the **top ten most popular and fastest-growing words or phrases being tweeted about at any given moment.**

Twitter refreshes this list constantly, so the trending topics reflect things people are most intensely interested in. It often reveals breaking news before mainstream media; Michael Jackson's death, for instance, trended almost instantly. On the more frivolous end, it usually includes jokey hashtags people bat around. Because the list values velocity over volume, popular topics sometimes disappear as they age, even when they still draw lots of tweets.

Here you can see that at the moment of this screenshot, people in the U.S. were talking about things like George Lucas (who had tweaked *Star Wars* for its Blu-ray debut); MSG ANNIVERSARY (a Justin Bieber–related issue); #ThingsWeNeedToChange (a mostly civic-minded hashtag); and #replacebooktitleswithbacon ("Eat, Pray, Bacon").

You can find Trends on the right side of your Twitter page (if you're not logged in, you can see them at http://twitter.com/search). One of the nifty things about Trends is that Twitter lets you choose a geographic area for them. The default setting is Worldwide. But the little "change" link brings up a list of countries, and when you pick one, you often get a list of cities within the country, too. This feature is handy when, for example, you want to see whether the UK and the US (or London and New York) are responding differently to an event like the riots in London. It can also be useful to keep an eye on trending topics in a particular region—your area or another you're interested in—just to stay connected with what other people there are paying attention to. In Chapter 2, we share tools for tracking trends.

@whitneyhess
Whitney Hess

Hello Portland! Tweetup tomorrow (Mon) 6pm at Green Dragon. Don't miss it. Spread the word and bring friends. I like meeting new people :)

4 Apr via SocialScope   ☆ Favorite   ⇄ Retweet   ↰ Reply

@zoecello
Zoe Keating ✓

coming to #SFMusicTech on Sept 12? if you are, wanna tweetup at lunch and talk shop? bit.ly/1rQpnB

19 hours ago via TweetDeck   ☆ Favorite   ⇄ Retweet   ↰ Reply

@Braves
Atlanta Braves ✓

Braves TweetUp is this THURSDAY. We're talking Q&A w/@KrisMedlen54 + @Jim_Powell, TweetUp shirts + more! Get tix now:atmlb.com/phRZFX

22 hours ago via Social Marketing Hub   ☆ Favorite   ⇄ Retweet   ↰ Reply

Key Twitter jargon: tweetup

Preplanned or spontaneous, a "tweetup" is an in-person gathering organized largely via Twitter. Whether social, professional or for a cause, **a tweetup often brings together people who previously knew each other only on Twitter.** Such events are very satisfying, as the face-to-face meetings can spark new connections.

Even better, because messages on Twitter are public, tweetups can draw a mix of people who don't already know each other (even on Twitter), generating new connections. As you see here, a tweetup can be pretty casual or fairly organized, and lots of people use them when they travel to meet others.

For help pulling together a large tweetup, consider **Twtvite** (http://twtvite.com).

twitter tip

Of course, part of the charm in a tweetup is that you can all tweet about the event as it transpires. Make sure to designate a hashtag, described earlier in this chapter, to group everyone's messages.

twitter

Twitter is over capacity.

Too many tweets! Please wait a moment and try again.

56

Twitter jargon: Fail Whale

In its first few years, Twitter grew quickly—more quickly than the company could keep pace with. As a result, the service conked out a lot. How often? Often enough to have **its own logo for downtime.** Infamously known as the "Fail Whale," it appeared on the screen when Twitter was over capacity.

Twitter still has occasional hiccups, but it's now much more reliable, and the Fail Whale is now an endangered species. We mention it here mostly out of fondness for the image and respect for its oft-noted past.

Little-known fact: the whale was designed by Yiying Lu (@YiyingLu), who posted it to iStockPhoto, where Twitter co-founder Biz Stone came across it. Lu has since taken the image down from iStockPhoto, but you can see more of her illustrations at http://yiyinglu.com.

58

Why I Love Twitter

Sat
Nov 29
2008

by Tim O'Reilly | comments: 95

listen ◄))

If you care what I think, you know that Twitter is just about the best way to learn 🖳 what I'm paying attention to. I pass along tidbits of O'Reilly news, interesting reading from mailing lists and blogs I follow, and of course, tidbits from the twitterers I'm following. These are all the things I could never find time to put on my blog, but that I spray via email like a firehose at editors, conference planners, and researchers within O'Reilly. A lot of my job is, as we say, "redistributing the future" - following interesting people, and passing on what I learn to others. And twitter is an awesome tool for doing just that.

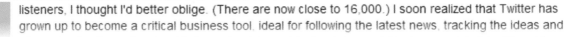

Like a lot of people, I tried out Twitter early on, but didn't stick to it. M~~e~~
~~conversation was personal, and I didn't have time for it. I came back~~

listeners, I thought I'd better oblige. (There are now close to 16,000.) I soon realized that Twitter has grown up to become a critical business tool, ideal for following the latest news, tracking the ideas and

Try it for three weeks or your money back—guaranteed!

People often say that they dip into Twitter once or twice and don't get it. Which is understandable since the real value of Twitter becomes evident only after you've followed a few accounts for a while and have absorbed their rhythms.

If you're having trouble seeing what all the fuss is about, try this tactic: follow at least a few promising accounts, and then for three weeks, log into Twitter daily, catch up on messages and click around for five to ten minutes. Every few days, make sure to check the trending topics (described in Chapter 1). Finally, spend 30 minutes one day running a few searches (described in Chapter 2) to see what you can learn from the discussions on Twitter.

At the end of three weeks, you'll have spent five hours total giving a fair shake to the most important new communications tool we've seen since email. (If it still doesn't work for you, pass this book along to a friend.)

Support ✓

@Support Twitter HQ
Twitter Support Team. Follow and DM us with questions.
We're here to help Mon - Fri from 8am to 6pm PST.
http://support.twitter.com

Tweet to @Support

Tweets   Favorites   Following ▾   Followers ▾   Lists ▾

Support Support
Some users have reported that they are not seeing their Mentions.
Engineers are aware - thanks everyone for letting @Support know!
1 hour ago

Support Support
Please spread the word: do NOT click links that claim to have photo
albums of you and NEVER give out your password.
support.twitter.com/articles/76036...
24 Aug

Support Support
Need help on an iPhone, BlackBerry, or Android? #Didyouknow you
can access our Help Center on your device? support.twitter.com
Cell-ebrate!
24 Aug

Get help from Twitter

Twitter has hundreds of employees and hundreds of millions of users. Given that ratio, the company does a remarkable job of providing support. Here are their **primary help channels:**

1. Twitter's help pages (http://support.twitter.com) are pretty clear and comprehensive. They include good explanations, descriptions of known problems, troubleshooting tips and a place to file or check on the status of a support request (including help with hacked or unexpectedly blocked accounts).

2. The Twitter **@Support account** (http://twitter.com/support), shown here, provides updates and tips.

3. The Twitter **Status blog** (http://status.twitter.com) reports on hiccups, outages and other service issues.

4. Get Satisfaction hosts forums where people discuss Twitter help topics: http://getsatisfaction.com/twitter.

CHAPTER 2 | Listen In

Twitter gives you two superhero strengths everyone wants: the power to read people's thoughts and the ability to overhear conversations as if you were a fly on the wall.

To get those bionic senses, you need the right tools and a few search skills. In this chapter, we give you a guided tour of essential listening on Twitter—the who, what, where, why and how.

← Back to Home

Save this search

Results for "organic food"

Tweets · Top ▾   Refine results »

---

20 new tweets

Colorado Colorado Tourism ⟲ 5 Retweets
Colorado's restaurants embodied the locally grown, fresh-**food**
movement long before it was popular to do so: http://bit.ly/7hW9S
25 Jul
↗ Promoted by Colorado Tourism

---

thetravelchica The Travel Chica
The Best Places to Eat **Organic Food** in Buenos Aires, Argentina
http://ow.ly/6foZW via @argentowine
11 hours ago
✉ Retweeted 3 times

---

ecogreen4us ecogreen4us
Organic products help us sustaining our environment as well as
build healthier lifestyle. lnk.ms/R7Ltk
11 hours ago

ClayEnos Clay Enos
I love this for who owns what as much as for who says what: Nestle
wants you to be scared of **organic food**: grist.org/**organic-food**/2…
via @grist
11 hours ago

OrganicPortal

Use Twitter search

Because people tweet about the things they do, encounter, read and think, the site is **a goldmine of ideas, feelings and conversations.**

To become a fly on the wall, head to Twitter's search box, which lives at the top of the site. (If you want to search without logging in, head instead to http://twitter.com/search.) You can see on the opposite page that a search for the phrase "organic food" brings up a slew of results with people discussing articles about the topic. If search results include photos or video, those appear to the right of the tweets.

As people post to Twitter, their messages get added to search results *instantly*. Twitter lets you know fresh updates are available by posting a little message at the top of your screen— here, "20 new tweets," which appeared seconds after the first set of results. (See that the top result here is "Promoted by Colorado Tourism"? We discuss Promoted Tweets in Chapter 6.)

Note the word "Top" at the beginning of the results. It indicates that Twitter has filtered the results by an algorithm that determines popularity. The tradeoff is that popular results push down most recent results. If you want all of the results, or just those that include links (if, say, you're looking for pointers to a deeper discussion), just click the little arrow next to Top to get those options.

Finally, keep in mind that like many search services, Twitter lets you use a few simple, powerful search tricks. To search for a phrase, put quotes around it, as we do here. To remove a search term, put the minus sign (-) in front of it. To search for either of two terms, put the word "or" between them.

twitter Search 🔍 Home Profile Messages W

← Back to Home ⊕ Save this search

Tre
#Ja
#yo
#S

Results for power from:corybooker include:retweets

Tweets · All ▾

Refine results »

Ha
Chr
CJ2
Sep
Lab
Chr
En

 CoryBooker Cory Booker ⑤
On Bock Ave in the South Ward now. Folks here don't have **power** either. Good to see our police out stationed in every blacked out area.
15 hours ago ☆ Favorite ↻ Retweet ↩ Reply

Abc
Sho
Res

 CoryBooker Cory Booker
AWESOME, Thanks 2 PSE&G RT @rockout973 Thanks, as promised trees & **power** situation rectified by midnight like u promised. #Underwood street
31 Aug

 CoryBooker Cory Booker
On Bock Ave in the South Ward now. Folks here don't have **power** either. Good to see our police out stationed in every blacked out area.
30 Aug

 CoryBooker Cory Booker
On Crescent & Keer ave now. Heard frustrations of folks who need power for their medical conditions. Folks going into day 4 with no

Take advantage of advanced search

Twitter's **advanced search is one of the best—and most underused—parts of the service.** To find it, head to http://twitter.com/search-advanced.

You get a form that looks like any old advanced search. But don't be fooled. It actually has several very cool options that you won't find in almost any other search—and they make Twitter search ultra-powerful.

Although these fields may look mundane, don't miss the fact that you can search for tweets to, from or mentioning specific accounts. You can also do a search for tweets from a certain location (the location is based on info people give in their bios, so it can be hazy). And you can look for people asking questions. The search results shown here are from Newark, NJ mayor Cory Booker (@CoryBooker) talking about power (after Hurricane Irene).

twitter tip

Twitter search (advanced and plain old) goes back just a few days or weeks, depending on what you're looking for. If you need older search results, try the search tools described a little later in this chapter.

twitter

Kaiser -Chiefs -roll -George 🔍 Home Profile Messages Wh

← Back to Home

⊕ **Save this search**

Results for Kaiser -Chiefs -roll -George

Tweets · Top ▾   Refine results »

virginiagriffey Virginia Griffey   ⧉
I'm at **Kaiser** Permanente Medical Center - Richmond (901 Nevin
Ave, at Harbor Way, Richmond) 4sq.com/oGOmYv
11 minutes ago

InternAlert Dwayne Callis
RT @bsc_cleveland: Staff Pharmacist - **Kaiser** Permanente -
Parma, OH: pharmacy interns and technicians. Shares equally in...
based ......
15 minutes ago

SASanalytics SASanalytics
"Numbers Rule Your World," literally, acc. to author **Kaiser** Fung
bit.ly/nrOg3g #BA #allanalytics
21 minutes ago

readyfuels lauren   ⧉ ⚲
Physical therapy for my jaw - finally! (@ **Kaiser** Permanente - Park
Shadelands) 4sq.com/natzoB
25 minutes ago

HolyFoolErik ☩ Erik ☩

Four important things to search for

If you want really useful search results from Twitter, you have to spend some time playing with the advanced search options to figure out the relevant terms and topics people are talking about. Here are four topics to get you started:

1. Your name. It may be known as a "vanity search," but keeping an eye on what people say about you is a smart idea. (Don't forget that putting quotes around your name can help refine the results. Search for *"Jane Doe"* instead of *Jane Doe.*)

2. Your Twitter account name. Don't miss messages to or about you.

3. Your company, brand or product. Peek into the minds of customers, competitors, journalists and other key constituents. If you're a local business, use the advanced search "Location" option to narrow down results. Also, if your company name is common, use the minus sign to weed out inappropriate results. For instance, if you work for Kaiser Permanente, search for *Kaiser –Chiefs –roll -George* written in English to make sure messages about the band, the food item, the billionaire and German tweets don't overwhelm your results. (Here, a targeted search yields relevant results, with three of the top four results about Kaiser Permanente.)

4. Your competitors. Get market intel and ideas.

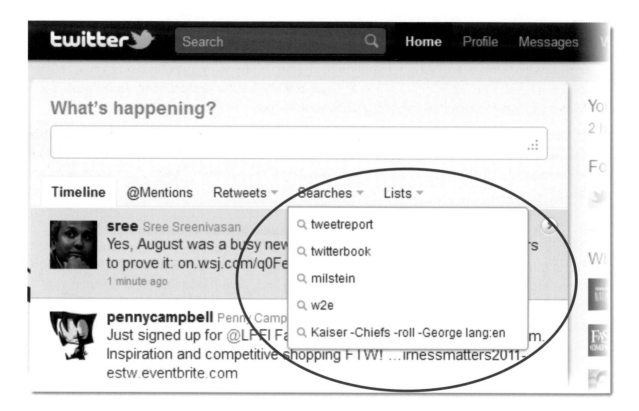

Save searches

So you've spent time tinkering with Twitter search, and you've figured out a few queries that bring up useful results. Do you have to head over to Twitter search every hour and type them in to see if you've got fresh messages? Of course not.

The most basic way to keep on top of searches is to run a search, and then look near the top of the results for the **"Save this search"** button. Once you click it, it changes to "Delete this saved search." To find your saved searches, head to your home page, and then look for the Searches tab. Click it to get a list of your saved searches, each of which is a link to a fresh search on that query.

Of course, it works with simple queries, too, like the results for a search on your name.

To delete a saved search, first run it, and then look near the top of the results for a red "x" marked "Remove saved search."

Track search with email alerts

Saved searches are all well and good if you spend half your time in Twitter. But what if you don't use it every day and still want to keep track of certain conversations? No problem. **Twilert** has you covered.

Twilert (http://twilert.com) will shoot you an **email message with an hourly or daily digest of tweets** that contain your search terms. It's like Google Alerts, only for Twitter instead of the rest of the web.

We've tailored the alert here to deliver messages about O'Reilly Media, while filtering out those about Bill O'Reilly (no relation).

Google

site:twitter.com/maddow budget 🎤

5 results (0.15 seconds)

🔍 Everything

📷 Images

🎬 Videos

📰 News

🛍 Shopping

More

San Francisco, CA
Change location

Show search tools

▸ Twitter / Rachel Maddow MSNBC: Breaking News about the su ... +1 🔍
twitter.com/maddow/status/56541493502033921
Breaking News about the supposed **budget** deal killed tonight's Cocktail Moment. Did one with the staff instead. #VeryFringeBenefit.

Twitter / Rachel Maddow MSNBC: Also... what's a non-fisca ... +1 🔍
twitter.com/maddow/status/45630213643702272 - Cached
Also... what's a non-fiscal **budget** bill? ... Also... what's a non-fiscal **budget** bill? 3:41 PM Mar 9th via web Retweeted by 100+ people. maddow. Rachel Maddow ...

Twitter / Rachel Maddow MSNBC: SecDef Gates makes forehea ... +1 🔍
https://twitter.com/maddow/status/2692831847
SecDef Gates makes forehead-smacking good arguments about the idiocy of the defense **budget**: http://is.gd/1CoSw 11:25 AM Jul 17th, 2009 via web ...

Twitter / Rachel Maddow MSNBC: Remember that wicked scary ... +1 🔍
twitter.com/maddow/status/1256789934
Remember that wicked scary job loss chart? Here it is among **budget** docs with some of its wicked scary chart friends (pdf!) http://is.gd/l1AJ.

Twitter / Rachel Maddow MSNBC: "the real path to a lower ... +1 🔍
twitter.com/maddow/status/5358777880551424

Hunt down—and back up—older tweets

Twitter is designed to help you find out what's happening right now, and you may have noticed that **it's hard to find old tweets—yours or anyone else's.** You can, however, employ a few search tricks, and you can back up your tweets, making them easier to access in the future.

To scroll back through your last 3,200 posts, head to the top of your home page and click "Your Tweets." To see somebody else's last 3,200 messages, simply go to their page.

Of course, manually sifting through messages is inefficient. This is where third-party tools come in. **Topsy** (http://topsy.com) says its archive goes back to May 2008 (narrow the search to Twitter by clicking the Tweets link at the top of the page, use the filter on the left side of the page to narrow the timeframe of results). **ReSearch.ly** (http://research.ly) says it goes back 1,000 days. (We cover two more archive searches on the next page.)

The major search engines also sometimes hit old gold. Try Googling with a query like this: *site:twitter.com/username keyword* (swap in the username of the person who tweeted and a keyword from the tweet, as shown here). Bing occasionally delivers, too.

For better access moving forward, back up your tweets. **TweetBackUp** (http://tweetbackup.com), offered by Backupity, is free and has active support on Twitter itself (@TweetBackUp). Once you've signed in (it uses your Twitter account for authentication, explained later in this chapter), it automatically backs up your tweets, and you can quickly export your last 3,200 tweets into any of four formats (which you can then search—and save to your own drives). As a bonus, the HTML and CSV formats give you the permanent URL for each tweet (described in Chapter 4).

SnapBird

@SARAHM AUTHENTICATED

Search beyond Twitter's history

SEARCH | Your friends' tweets ⌄

YOU | @SarahM

FOR | libya

FIND IT!

Searching *SarahM's friends' tweets* for **libya**

evanchill Was taking this piece on #Libya seriously until it got to the part about Gaddafi not really intending to hurt civilians. http://ow.ly/6j9zX
8:32 PM Sep 1th from HootSuite

evanchill Was just recalling the story in east #Libya months ago that dozens of female Colombian Gaddafi snipers were captured. Such rumors, this war
7:26 PM Sep 1th from HootSuite

NickKristof RT @brhone: "Without America, we would not be celebrating. We would be in the cemetery." **Libya**n to @NickKristof http://t.co/MxumFmw
6:51 PM Sep 1th from TweetDeck

NickKristof **Libya**n rebels are allowing ordinary Qaddafi loyalist families to flee to Tunisia. Rather a good sign, I think.
6:46 PM Sep 1th from web

evanchill Some shots I took inside Gaddafi's military intelligence compound in #Tripoli. http://ow.ly/6j1Ma #**Libya**
6:21 PM Sep 1th from HootSuite

Snap Bird has matched
5 tweets
out of
163 searched
dating back to the **afternoon** of
Sep 1th

PERMALINK

163 tweets searched.

Haven't found what you're looking for?

Search next 1,000 tweets

Search the nooks, crannies and archives of your account

As described earlier in this chapter, Twitter's own search service is useful, but it's limited. It goes back just a few days (sometimes less) and even the advanced search won't look in all the parts of your account you might want to access. **When you want to search tweets just from people you follow, or the tweets you've favorited (described later in this chapter), or your DMs (described in** Chapter 1**), you need a more refined tool.**

Snapbird (http://snapbird.org) is one option for these deep dives. It builds an archive of your account and then lets you cut a search in several useful ways. Here you can see a keyword search among tweets from people Sarah follows—a nice way to narrow down the barrage of sentiment on a topic and get a sense for what your followees' are thinking. You can also search favorites (yours or anyone else's) and DMs you've sent or received. The archive can be limited, but it's a good start.

Along the same lines, **PostPost** (http://postpo.st) lets you search your tweets and those of people you follow—and its archive generally goes back pretty far.

CloudMagic (http://cloudmagic.com), a browser extension for Chrome and Firefox, searches your incoming and outgoing messages. It's not clear how far back the archive goes, and it's not thorough (sometimes the results appear to include incoming messages; other times, not so much). But it is quick, and its search services for Gmail and Google Apps are quite good, so perhaps this will improve.

Left panel:

| Yankees OR NYY OR Yanks | Search! | Stop |

Settings ⊕

TweetFireApp: From the creator of TweetGrid, a blazing fast new Twitter client for iPhone - TweetFire - http://TweetFireApp.com/

Advertisement from TweetGrid

JonathanHoo: Montero DHing tonight just made the @yankees game worth watching.

Thu Sep 01 - 3:47:49 pm

Vitale724: @russellmartin55 We will If AJ pitches like we ALL know he is capable of!!! GO YANKEES!!!

Thu Sep 01 - 3:47:49 pm

OmarSalima11: RT @Vboccone: #MLB. Hasta ahora 3 criollos han subido a la MLB con la expansión de rosters: JC Boscán (#Bravos), F.Doubront (#RedSox) y J.Montero (#NYY)

Thu Sep 01 - 3:47:47 pm

Mike_aggmoney: @Yankees we need A-rod for tonight if AJ is pitching -__-

Thu Sep 01 - 3:47:46 pm

MARIALEOROPEZA: RT @Cornielle1346: Yankees Jeter SS, Granderson CF, Teixeira 1B, Canó 2B, Swisher RF, Jones LF, MONTERO DH, Martin C, Núñez 3B, Burnett P.

Thu Sep 01 - 3:47:45 pm

metsyankees00: @SVTSport Ni måste kolla upp uttalet på Carmelita Jeter. New York Yankees lagkapten sedan 16 år heter Derek Jeter. Uttalas "jiitoer".

Thu Sep 01 - 3:47:40 pm

prettyboyskip: @russellmartin55 that's what I'm talking about f*ck Boston

Right panel:

| Jeter | Search! | Stop |

Settings ⊕

LVADone: RT @YankeesPR: New DH...Tonight's lineup @ BOS: Jeter 6, Granderson 8, Teixeira 3, Cano 4, Swisher 9, Jones 7, Montero DH, Martin 2, Nunez 5, Burnett 1

Thu Sep 01 - 3:48:42 pm

YOHANTV: Spoke too soon. Tonight's Lineup: Derek Jeter SS Curtis Granderson CF Mark Teixeira 1B Robinson Cano 2B Nic... (cont) http://t.co/U9VV4Of

Thu Sep 01 - 3:48:41 pm

KobeShrug: RT @Yankees: Montero in 9/1 lineup: Jeter SS, Granderson CF, Teixeira 1B, Cano 2B, Swisher RF, Jones LF, Montero DH, Martin C, Nunez 3B, Burnett P

Thu Sep 01 - 3:48:39 pm

boomerangdrinks: alineacion yankee jeter granderson texeira cano swisher jones montero dh martin nunez burnett

Thu Sep 01 - 3:48:38 pm

dyanitab: RT @YankeesPR: New DH...Tonight's lineup @ BOS: Jeter 6, Granderson 8, Teixeira 3, Cano 4, Swisher 9, Jones 7, Montero DH, Martin 2, Nunez 5, Burnett 1

Thu Sep 01 - 3:48:28 pm

HartyLFC: RT @Yankees: Montero in 9/1 lineup: Jeter SS, Granderson CF, Teixeira 1B, Cano 2B, Swisher RF, Jones LF, Montero DH, Martin C, Nunez 3B, Burnett P

Thu Sep 01 - 3:48:24 pm

mong82191: JESUS IS HERE!!!! RT @Yankees: Montero in 9/1 lineup: Jeter SS, Granderson CF, Teixeira 1B, Cano 2B, Swisher (cont) http://t.co/KzTixKY

Thu Sep 01 - 3:48:24 pm

Stay on top of several searches at once, including live-event coverage

When you want to see what people are saying about several topics at once, and you want to watch the conversations in real-time, try a service like **TweetGrid** (http://tweetgrid.com), shown here, or **Monitter** (http://monitter.com).

These services are useful not only for seeing what people are saying, but also for getting a sense of the speed and volume of tweets on different topics. **And they're particularly useful for tracking live events,** where people might use a couple of hashtags or different terms to tweet about the proceedings.

If you find yourself keeping an eye on the same searches every day, consider using Twitter via a client like TweetDeck, which lets you easily save and see searches. We describe third-party programs later in this chapter.

twitter tip

For services that let you include a complex query, here's an easy way to get the search string. Use Twitter's advanced search to run your query. At the top of the results page, you'll see your query converted into a search string (something like Yankees OR Yanks near:"New York, NY" within:25mi). Paste it into your current app.

TOPSY

91
posts

TOP ★5K

tweet

Language
▶ **All languages**
English

Essential Summer Dishes - Interactive Feature - NYTimes.com

nytimes.com/interactive/2011/08/31/dining/20110831-summer-cooking.html - view page - cached page

Some flavors belong so completely to the season that, if you haven't tasted them at least once before Labor Day, you haven't really had a summer. Below, five writers share their memories and recipes for the one warm-weather dish they consider essential eating.

#food   #summer   #cooking   #recipes   #diningwine   #nytimesdiningsection   #diningin

Interesting posts about this link

kimseverson: @virginiawillis @nytimesfood Thanks for sharing your field pea story. Can I come sit on your porch? http://t.co/7jqksdO
2 days ago 4 similar tweets Highly Influential retweet

nytimesdining: Summer Essentials: Grilled Marinated Flank Steak http://t.co/zmUqpIf
2 days ago 3 similar tweets Highly Influential retweet

virginiawillis: Last tastes of summer. Field Peas from "V Willis" via @kimseverson in @nytimesfood. Glad to share my summer memory. http://t.co/i73IfIF
2 days ago 2 similar tweets retweet

virginiawillis: Pretty doggone excited about being in the @nytimesfood today with Last Tastes of Summer! http://t.co/CIdwtCh
2 days ago 2 similar tweets retweet

finewinedine: 5 NY Times writers share their memories and recipes of favourite warm weather dishes http://t.co/58LLBAn #recipes #summer
2 days ago 2 similar tweets retweet

samsifton: Whole bunch of good summer recipes and yams from D1 peeps: http://t.co/VyPfYzw. And a call for

Track tweeted links to your website

If you're trying to keep track of tweets that link to your website, you've got a tricky problem. Because people use URL shorteners to create links compact enough to fit in a tweet, **you can't simply search for mentions of your domain.**

Luckily, **Topsy** (http://topsy.com) has your back. Just type in the URL you want to track—either the original link or a shortened version—and it pulls up a list of appropriate results. You can search for links to a domain name (like nytimes.com) or to a specific page, as we've shown here (http://www.nytimes.com/interactive/2011/08/31/dining/20110831-summer-cooking.html).

To keep a regular eye on your results, grab the RSS feed or get email alerts for your search; both options are on the right side of the page.

twitter tip

Topsy doesn't work with secure URLs (i.e., those that start with *https*). Often, though, you can just remove the "s" at the end, so the URL starts *http*, and you're good to go.

twopular

trends on **twitter** aggregator

| now | 2 hours | 8 hours | day | week | month | year |

trends on **twitter** right now

1. #replacebooktitleswithbacon 1.35 ▶ 🔳 ⌂ Ⓖ ✍
2. #ThingsWeNeedToChange 8.00 ▶ 🔳 ⌂ Ⓖ ✍
3. Hello September 9.35 ▶ 🔳 ⌂ Ⓖ ✍
4. #WhyYoBaby 9.25 ▶ 🔳 ⌂ Ⓖ ✍
5. Goodbye August 8.35 ▶ 🔳 ⌂ Ⓖ ✍

6. WHY KHLEO THOMAS 1.30 ▶ 🔳 ⌂ Ⓖ ✍
7. Botafogo 2 x 0 Palmeiras 0.10 ▶ 🔳 ⌂ Ⓖ ✍
8. Rodrigo Alvim 0.35 ▶ 🔳 ⌂ Ⓖ ✍
9. MSG ANNIVERSARY 13.15 ▶ 🔳 ⌂ Ⓖ ✍
10. Wade Belak 4.00 ▶ 🔳 ⌂ Ⓖ ✍

twitter live search:

press ▶ in the trend list above to load the latest tweets for a trend

Dig deeper on trending topics

The trending topics, described in Chapter 1, are all well and good when you can tell what they're about (*Glee*, earthquake, Bieber). But **what about the cryptic terms?** (AGT, #w2e, Frimpong.)

Often you can decipher a topic by clicking through and reading a handful of tweets that include it. In other cases, a quick Google search does the trick. When those methods fail, try **What the Trend** (http://whatthetrend.com), which lists trending topics, along with a brief description of each. If there's no explanation yet for a topic, the site invites you to add one, assuming someone will know the story. You can also edit existing topics. Caveat: What the Trend is not always up to date.

Another useful tool for understanding trends is **Twopular** (http://twopular.com), shown here. It gives you the trending topics now, or for the last two hours, eight hours, day, week, month or year. It's handy not only because it **gives you snapshots over time,** but also because it tells you for how many hours a topic trended (check the number to the right of each trend).

In Chapter 6, we cover **Trendistic** (http://trendistic.com), which compares and graphs trends.

tweetmeme v2 Hottest Links on Twitter

All   News   Images   Videos

Everything

Most Recent | Top in 24 Hours | Top in 7 Days

---

559 tweets
retweet

Storyteller App Turns Facebook Posts Into Sponsored Stories [PICS]

MASHABLE.COM - Social brand marketing service Wildfire has launched a Facebook App focused on creating better content for Facebook's Sponsored Stories.Facebook launched Sponsored Stories in January and pitched it as a more social and engaging ad format. Brands...

ContentLawyer   0 Comments   Report   Made Popular 43 mins ago

---

269 tweets
retweet

U-KISS' 2nd album, 'Neverland', places first right after its release

ALLKPOP.COM - It's been revealed that U-KISS's 2nd album, 'Neverland', topped the Hanteo Charts immediately after its release!On September 1st, U-KISS placed 1st on Hanteo Charts, overcoming the explosive popularity of Super Junior and Leessang. The...

Smartasspenguin   0 Comments   Report   Made Popular 1 hour ago

---

Socialsafe.net

1746 tweets
retweet

"SocialSafe: Your social journal treasured forever"

SOCIALSAFE.NET - "Use @SocialSafe to regularly download Facebook & Twitter, creating your social journal treasured forever. Private, searchable & offline".

---

*

220 tweets

The 20 Most-Shared Video Ads This Month

MASHABLE.COM - It's a safe bet that Ken Block, a professional rally driver, and Danny MacAskill, a Scottish cyclist, are obscure to

Find out what people are reading

Because people like to tweet links to interesting things they've read, **Twitter can be your filtered news portal.** A lot of the time, though, the people you follow will serve up more juicy reading material than you can ingest.

If you want a snapshot of the most popular stories being passed around Twitter, **TweetMeme** (http://tweetmeme.com), shown here, can give you insight. It tracks and ranks the URLs flying through the Twittersphere, showing the most popular links and how many times each has appeared in a tweet. Of course, you can sort by most recent, the past 24 hours or the past week. And the site also lets you explore by category.

If you use an tablet, try a nifty app that aggregates content from Twitter. For the iPad, **Flipboard** (http://flipboard.com) and **Zite** (http://zite.com) are good choices; **Pulse** (http://pulse.me) works on Android devices and the iPhone, too. **News.me** (http://news.me) is available as an iPad app or a daily email. These apps open the links in your incoming timeline, turning your Twitter reading into an amazing multimedia experience; think of it as a next-generation social newspaper. This really is the future of news, and if you don't already have a tablet, it could well be the excuse you've needed to get one.

#LeanStartup Bundle: ericri.es/pH1juW
23 minutes ago

dontgetcaught Denise Graveline
Famous Speech Friday: Michelle Obama's speech to young African women leaders bit.ly/qwrcTr on The Eloquent Woman
27 minutes ago ☆ Favorite ⇄ Retweet ↩ Reply

baratunde Baratunde
Having a great discussion about #howtobeblack w black

Bookmark links for later reading and draw attention to tweets now

Twitter has a Favorites feature. You can use it to collect funny or insightful posts, and it's also **a good way to bookmark things you want to read later.** When you mouse over a message, a star appears underneath it with the word "Favorite", as shown here; click that to add the post to your list of favorites. To find your faves, head to the top of your account page, and click Profile and then the Favorites tab (look beneath your bio). Twitter stores up to 3,200 favorites, so if you find yourself hitting the limit, you can unfavorite tweets by mousing over them and clicking the gold star that appears.

Favoriting can be especially handy when you're on the road using your phone, and you want to save a link to read later on a bigger screen. If you're using a mobile client (discussed later in this chapter), click around to find the built-in favorite feature.

In Chapter 4, we talk about using Favorites to draw attention to tweets.

twitter

You can use your Twitter account to sign in to other sites and services.
By signing in here, you can use PostPost without sharing your Twitter password.

Authorize PostPost to use your account?

This application will be able to:

- Read Tweets from your timeline.
- See who you follow.

| SarahM |
| Password |

Forgot your password?

Sign In **Cancel**

This application **will not be able to**:

- Follow new people.
- Update your profile.
- Post Tweets for you.
- Access your direct messages.
- See your Twitter password.

PostPost
By Boathouse
postpo.st

The Twitter strip search tool. We strip out the noise by delivering realtime and historical search results only from the people you follow.

← Cancel, and return to app

Use a life-changing third-party program

The Twitter web interface is decent, but frankly, it lacks features and flexibility. The good news is that you have alternatives. Thanks to the way Twitter shares its data (for you geeks, that's their API), other people have created programs that let you access your account. And a lot of these third-party clients are better for power users than the Twitter website itself.

If you use Twitter regularly, like, say, more than once a week, consider trying **a program that can make your sending, receiving and listening more effective.** With just a few minutes of setup, they can take your tweeting from tedious to life-changing.

On the next pages, we describe a couple of our favorites. They come in two flavors: desktop and browser-based. The choice is a matter of personal preference—and also whether they work with your operating system. You might try one of each to decide which is best for you.

twitter tip

Many third-party programs require that you share your Twitter password. It's safe to do so with Twitter's authentication system. Look for a button that says, "Sign in with Twitter" or similar, which takes you to a Twitter form like this. Fill it out and click "Sign In" to return to the original site, which won't have access to your password.

Seesmic

Home | Messages | Contacts | ⟳ | Click Here to Update your Status | 🔍 Search on Twitter

SarahM
- Home
- @ Mentions
- Sent
- ★ Favorite
- Direct messages
- Retweets
- Lists
  - Second
  - Top
  - lean startups ..
  - new york dog
  - @LindaStone/in..
  - New List
- 🔍 Searches
- Trending T...
  - #wordstodescri...
  - #SomebodyToldY..

90

⊞ Home / SarahM

⊕ http://t.co/ec...
4m ago via twitterfeed
↻ retweeted by craignewmark

slidesharegeeks DevOps
@slideshare ⊕ http://t.co/sg...
#devops #devopsdays
4m ago via web
↻ retweeted by jboutelle and 3 others

harryallen RT @metacritic:
Apollo 18 (Metascore->23)
NYDN: "Has no thrills, no chills,
no scares." BoxOffice: "Drab
horror." ⊕ http://t.co/zn...
4m ago via tGadget ⊠ 65

harryallen Higher Ed. RT
@TheAtlanticWire: A professor
accused of dealing meth seen
as "friendly, disorganized" by
students ⊕ http://t.co/3R...
4m ago via tGadget ⊠ 65

anildash Google Knol team to
Notebook product team: EAT IT
SUCKAZZZZZZ

@ Mentions / SarahM

bgreenlee @SarahM Very cool,
although I'd like something that
can function without the phone.
Something along the lines of
⊕ http://t.co/XD...
3h ago via Twitter for Mac in reply
to SarahM ⊠ 40

annmcharles TY and same! RT
@susanmcp1: Brilliance #FF
@LauraLeinweber
@DianaVerdeNieto
@celinecousteau @portergale
@sloane @endeavoringE
@SarahM...
3h ago via HootSuite ⊠ 44

ApplexStephen @SarahM Isn't it
sadder if they send him back?
5h ago via Twitter for
BlackBerry® in reply to SarahM
⊠ 46

kak_jie18 twitter: @SarahM hee.
She's really become a pro at all
modes of transport. And the look
always says, "Where does...
⊕ http://t.co/g9...
5h ago via twitterfeed ⊠ 21

⊞ List: @LindaStone/interestin...

brainpicker Heartbroken?
There's no app for that, but
there's a spa – in Germany
⊕ http://j.mp/o2...
12m ago via TweetDeck

ElinMllr Ssupercommittee to
hold first meeting next week
⊕ http://t.co/3P...
25m ago via TweetDeck

brainpicker So thrilled to see
doodler extraordinaire
@SunniBrown on CNN!
⊕ http://j.mp/pt... Her book is a
must ⊕ http://j.mp/gt... (via
@NancyGiordano)
27m ago via TweetDeck

brainpicker Wow – absolutely
amazing 3D-printed imaginative
jewelry on @Fab today
⊕ http://j.mp/oT... (I got the
honeycomb.)
42m ago via TweetDeck

carlacasilli Sometimes I think
that my Twtter follower count

Life-changing program #1: Seesmic

Seesmic (http://seesmic.com), available as a website or a desktop program, **is full of thoughtful features.** Both let you access an array of social media accounts, including Facebook, LinkedIn and Foursquare, creating a one-stop dashboard for your various activities. It's also worthy for Twitter alone (and it lets you add multiple Twitter accounts).

On the sending side, Seesmic is strong. For each incoming tweet, it gives you the standard options to reply, retweet, DM, mark as a favorite or report spam. It also lets you quote a tweet, reply to all or send the message to email. For fresh tweets, it has a built-in URL-shortening feature that lets you choose the compression service. Plus, it integrates with a couple of photo-sharing services and can transliterate Roman characters into other languages. One of Seesmic web's most popular options is the ability to schedule tweets—very handy when you're reading something mind-bending at 2 a.m. that you want to share at an hour your followers will likely see it. (Seesmic Desktop doesn't have a scheduling option.)

On the listening side, Seesmic shines. It lets you add or remove columns to track the activity you care about most (shown here, on Seesmic web: Sarah's incoming timeline, @mentions and a list). And you can temporarily mute individual followees if, say, they're tweeting too heavily from an event you don't care about. Seesmic also has a setting many consider magical: you can turn off auto-scroll, which means that when you slide down a column, the site holds your position as new tweets come in, thus letting you read in chronological order.

Seesmic Desktop's interface isn't quite as clear as its web sibling's, nor does it let you schedule tweets. But it does have some extra features, and it offers a bevy of plug-ins that let you add every conceivable kind of account, including eBay, Flickr, Yammer and more.

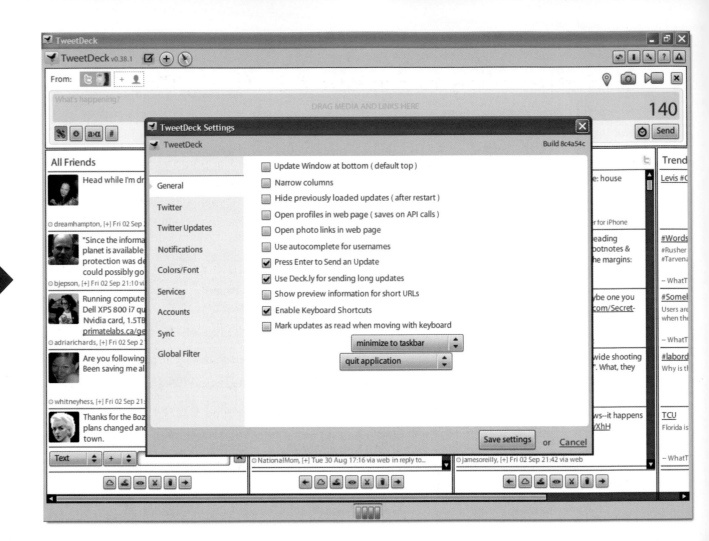

Life-changing program #2: TweetDeck

TweetDeck (http://tweetdeck.com), acquired by Twitter in May 2011, is a popular client, available as a desktop app or a website. It was the first third-party client to let you add columns for viewing different incoming streams, and it's retained a fan base over time, clocking in as the most popular way to access Twitter after Twitter.com. **The desktop version, in particular, is well thought out and highly customizable;** the browser-based version is not as appealing an option. Neither version has been updated frequently since the Twitter acquisition.

Like Seesmic, TweetDeck lets you sign into a slew of social media accounts, and you're also welcome to use it just for Twitter (it can handle multiple accounts). In addition to the options offered by Seesmic (including scheduled tweets and a saved position in your timeline), TweetDeck has a very useful feature to shorten tweets. It can automatically shorten URLs, and it also helps you take a webcam video and include that in a tweet. TweetDeck lets you filter incoming tweets in a handful of ways, and it has a world of useful settings, shown here, to tweak your tweeting experience. As you graduate to power user, rifle through these choices.

TweetDeck's desktop program runs on Adobe Air, which, depending on your computer's settings, may install automatically along with TweetDeck. If it doesn't, you can download and install it from http://bit.ly/getair; it takes just a minute. The software combo tends to suck up system resources, so if you notice your computer slowing down, you may want to close and restart TweetDeck (if not the whole machine).

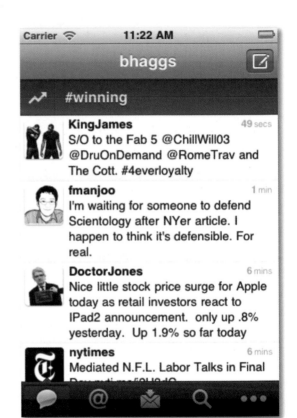

Use a great mobile client

A good deal of Twitter's appeal comes from the fact that you can **send and receive messages from anywhere you happen to be with your mobile phone or tablet.** Twitter's own mobile site, http://m.twitter.com, is fine but basic. If you want to amp up your listening on the road, try a dedicated mobile client. There are loads of apps to choose from for any given device, and we mention just a handful here. Keep in mind that if your first download doesn't feel like a winner, you have options. (We don't list URLs for these mobile clients because you can find them all through the relevant app stores.)

For iPhone, **Twitter for iPhone** is the official app (shown here with screenshots from the Twitter blog); in a past life, it was Tweetie, a popular third-party client that Twitter acquired in 2010. If you want alternatives, check out **Twitterific** or **Echofon**. For iPad, the winner is usually **Twitter for iPad**, though some prefer **Twitterific** or **Echofon**.

For Android devices, **Twitter for Android** is okay but can feel under-featured. You may want to try one of the appealing options from **Seesmic** or **TweetDeck**.

For BlackBerry, **Twitter for BlackBerry** is decent. But **UberSocial** is a strong contender, and Seesmic's app is worth trying.

Incidentally, you don't have to run the same mobile and desktop clients. It works totally fine to run, say, TweetDeck on your laptop and Twitterific on your iPhone. Some app makers, though (like Seesmic), will sync your accounts across devices, which can be important for power users.

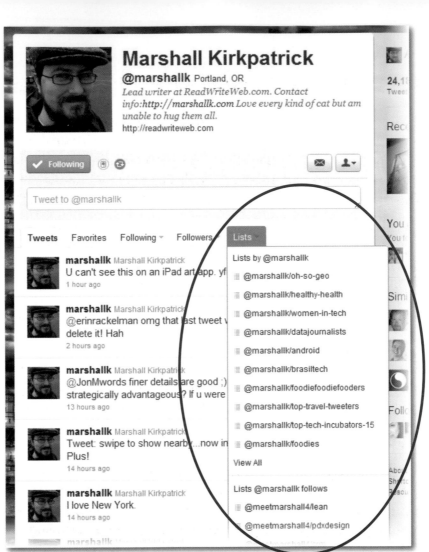

Follow smart people you don't know

You can use Twitter to stay in touch with friends and family. But **to get the most out of the service, follow at least a few people you don't already know.** They'll point out articles you wouldn't normally see. They'll give you a sense of what's important in another region, industry or social sphere. In addition, if you're using Twitter for professional reasons, following peers and thought leaders in your sector can help establish a connection.

There are a number of ways you can find smart, interesting people to follow. First, run a regular Twitter search, looking up a few terms that are important to you, and see who's sharing good ideas and links. You might then take a look at a searchable directory like **WeFollow** (http://wefollow.com), which organizes Twitterers by topic.

For a more powerful approach, use Twitter's list feature. Designed to let you group accounts into categories (like "food writers" or "my elected officials"), lists also help you discover people by topic, because *other* users create public lists. Here, for instance, are the lists Marshall Kirkpatrick (@marshallk) has created (shown the way you, not Marshall, would see them). When you click one, Twitter takes you to a page where you can choose to follow the list or sift through the accounts on it. Note that when you follow a list, the tweets in it don't show up in your main timeline. Instead, on your account page, go to the List tab and find "Lists you follow." (Later in this chapter, we explain how to create your own lists.)

Even better than clicking around are tools that find and create lists. **Listorious** (http://listorious.com) not only lists lists, it also provides a useful directory of accounts by common tags. **Plexus Engine** (http://plexusengine.com), described in more detail on the next page, does a great job finding key accounts by topic and compiling lists for you.

10 Most-Influential People*

1. Rafinha Bastos
Followers: **1,690,817**
Influence: **90**

2. Chad Ochocinco
Followers: **1,651,070**
Influence: **89**

3. Conan O'Brien
Followers: **2,367,928**
Influence: **88**

4. Stephen Fry
Followers: **2,188,395**
Influence: **87**

5. Ryan Seacrest
Followers: **3,880,840**
Influence: **86**

6. Snoop Dogg

10 Most Followed People

1. Lady Gaga
Followers: **7,941,444**
Influence: **41**

2. Justin Bieber
Followers: **7,032,265**
Influence: **67**

3. Britney Spears
Followers: **6,652,470**
Influence: **59**

4. Barack Obama
Followers: **6,531,868**
Influence: **83**

5. Ashton Kutcher
Followers: **6,261,483**
Influence: **68**

6. Kim Kardashian

Figure out who's influential on Twitter

Figuring out who's influential on Twitter looks straightforward—just see who has the most followers, which **Twitaholic** (http://twitaholic.com) will show you. But **don't be deceived:** because Twitter automatically recommends followees for new accounts, because spammers game the system, and because people behave in a variety of ways on Twitter (tweeting frequently or almost never, for example), the number of followers actually tells you very little about the value or influence of an account. The lists you see here are from a May 2011 *New York Times* story about the gap between influencers and followers (see http://bit.ly/nyt-influence for the full results and explanation).

If you want to take into account not just followers, but also retweets and other factors, you could consider **Twitalyzer** (http://twitalyzer.com); **PeerIndex** (http://peerindex.com); or **Klout** (http://klout.com). They each offer algorithmically derived scores for individual accounts to help gauge relative impact. Bear in mind that "influence" and "impact" are subjective ideas, and the scores on these sites don't offer much context. Indeed, there's debate among statisticians and other geeks about whether these scores are meaningful at all. We tend to agree with the skeptics. (We also dislike the tweets sent by Klout, described in Chapter 3.)

If you're looking for people who are respected on a *particular topic,* which is a more useful way to think about influence, you're better off with a tool like **Plexus Engine** (http://plexusengine.com). It finds key people of several stripes (for instance, most followed by topic insiders, and most followed overall) in subject areas you define, and it automatically generates Twitter lists you can follow (we explain lists earlier in this chapter).

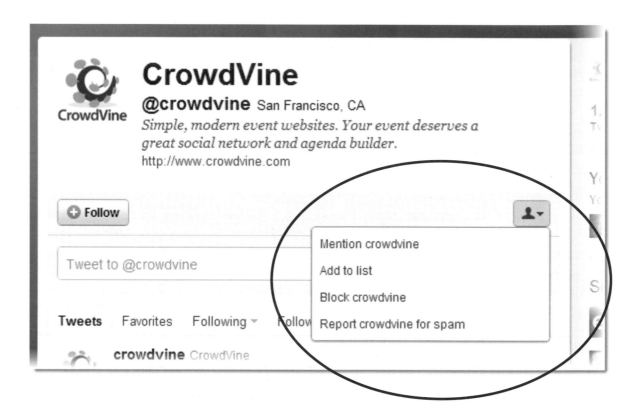

Keep track of friends and family

Following a flock of professional contacts and celebrities can make it hard to connect with friends and family on Twitter. Three easy ideas to **help you see their messages:**

1. Create a list for your high-priority accounts. Twitter lists let you group accounts into any category you choose, giving you a clean way to watch sub-groups of your followees. In this case, you might create a "Top Accounts" list. Head to your home page, find the Lists tab, and then click "Create a list." Twitter prompts you for a list name, and it also gives you the choice to make the list private—not a bad idea if this list names your most cherished friends and family. Next, Twitter lets you search for accounts to add. You can also add people from their account pages; find the little person icon shown here, and then click "Add to list."

You don't have to follow somebody to add them to a list, but if you aren't following them, you won't see their tweets in your main timeline; you'll see them only when you check the list (which you can find on your Lists tab). Removing an account from a list is simple but not obvious: head to the account page you want to remove, go through the "Add to list" procedure again, and uncheck the list name.

2. Get text updates just for the people whose messages you want to be certain you see (we cover Twitter-via-text in Chapter 1). When you follow somebody, you can see a teensy tiny little icon to the right of the Following button. The icon is a mobile phone, and when you click it, Twitter sends that account's updates to you via SMS. Bear in mind that your mobile carrier's SMS rates apply for incoming tweets, so be judicious in turning on this feature.

3. Create a private account and follow just your top people with it. Because you have to approve followers for private accounts, this a good choice for listen-only activity.

CHAPTER 3 | Hold Great Conversations

A lot of people find Twitter and think, "This is the perfect place to tell the world about myself!" After all, the site asks you, "What's happening?"

But it turns out that **Twitter isn't so much a broadcast medium as it is a discussion channel.** Indeed, the crux of social media is that it's not about you, your product or your story. It's about how you can add value to the communities that happen to include you. If you want to make a positive impact, forget about what you can get out of social media and start thinking about what you can contribute. Funnily enough, the more value you create for the community, the more value it will create for you.

In this chapter and the next, we show you how great conversationalists succeed and add value to their communities on Twitter.

@jamesbuck
James Buck
Arrested
10 Apr 08 via txt
Favorite
Retweet
Reply

Get great followers

If you want tons of followers on Twitter, you're not alone. But here's a secret: a small number of great followers is much more valuable than a herd of uninterested people. Think about it this way: if you're an accountant tweeting about tax tips, what's the point of having 1,000 followers if 999 of them are spam bots and war resistors who don't file taxes?

As a very practical example, when U.C. Berkeley graduate student James Buck (@jamesbuck) was on a trip to Egypt in April 2008 and tweeted that he'd been arrested, he had just 48 followers. But among them were friends who alerted the U.S. Embassy and the school, which worked to have him released. Lesson? Quality followers—i.e., people who care about you or your message—are worth more than a great quantity of random followers.

Drawing smart followers involves three key pieces:

1. Be interesting. The best way to become popular on Twitter is to post messages that other people want to read, retweet and respond to. In the next couple of chapters, we show how plenty of people are interesting and witty in 140 characters.

2. Be conversational. Engage with people, whether they're already following you or not. People like it. Plus, when prospective followers hit your Twitter account page, they'll see you're a friendly, thoughtful person.

3. Follow relevant people. If you follow somebody, there's a decent chance she'll follow you back. Use the tips in Chapter 2 to find people who are interested in the same sort of topics you are and follow them. It's the first step in building a relationship.

Reply to your @messages

As we explain in Chapter 1, a message that starts with *@YourUsername* is a public message to or about you. Sometimes those messages are a friendly hello or shout-out. Sometimes they're a question or comment. While **tweets don't carry quite as high an expectation of response as email messages do,** it's good community practice to respond to some if not all of them (with a message that starts or includes *@TheirUsername*).

Oddly, it can be tough to *find* your @messages. On your home page, click the @Mentions tab—*not* the Messages link—to discover these tweets. If you mouse over a message, a Reply swoosh appears; click that to respond. (Twitter automatically includes in the reply anyone @mentioned in the original tweet, so delete names if you're looking to respond only to the sender.) To send a fresh message to somebody, start with *@TheirUsername* or head to their account page, where Twitter provides a box for shooting them an @message, shown here.

twitter tip

If you receive a random @message from somebody you don't know, and it appears to be promoting something, it's probably spam. Later in this chapter, we explain how to report it.

@petersagal
Peter Sagal

RT @BobOnBusiness Retweeted by @MoRocca made my day. Now if @petersagal would, life would be complete. If not complete, at least less sucky.

26 Aug via Twittelator ☆ Favorite ⇄ Retweet ↩ Reply

@briansawyer
Brian Sawyer

Wow. RT @BostonTweet: Bruce Springsteen busking in Boston Public Garden yesterday while dropping his son off at BC: bit.ly/nGKIrh

2 Sep via TweetDeck ☆ Favorite ⇄ Retweet ↩ Reply

@elonjames
Elon James White

Thank you kindly. ;-) RT @NaijaRoyale: @elonjames I didn't know you were engaged. I'm hella late. Congratulations!

27 Aug via TweetDeck ☆ Favorite ⇄ Retweet ↩ Reply

Retweet clearly and classily: Part 1—the overview

As we describe in Chapter 1, **retweeting—or reposting somebody else's useful message and giving her credit—is one of the great Twitter conventions.** Trouble is, it's surprisingly hard to do. What if adding the retweeting info bumps you over 140 characters? What if you want to edit the message? What if you want to add your own comment?

The good news is that there are no rules, so you can't Do It Wrong. The even better news is that there are a few guidelines we can share, so you don't have to reinvent the retweet every time. The examples here show you what we believe are a couple of clear and classy retweets. The next few pages give you a roadmap for creating your own.

twitter tip

In order to make yourself more retweetable, make sure your messages leave room for somebody to add "RT @*YourUsername*". For example, on her personal account, Sarah often goes no higher than 130 characters (140 – 10 for "RT @SarahM").

What's happening?

Timeline   @Mentions   Retweets ▾   Searches ▾   Lists ▾

 barnaclebarnes Glen Barnes
Turned up at the house for a site visit Apparently our house supports
Tonga #RWC2011 yfrog.com/nv9jbwj
1 minute ago

 SLAMjamzRecords SLAMjamz Records ⟲ by harryallen
Need studio time? record at Terrordome Public Enemy Studio in
Roosevelt L.I contact juice 5166287069 for bookings
2 minutes ago

 thequote The Quote ⟲ by harryallen

Retweet clearly and classily: Part 2—retweets vs. quoted tweets

There are two primary ways you can retweet a message:

1. Hit the Retweet button in Twitter, which simply copies the tweet wholesale and makes it appear in your followers' timelines as it if came from the original writer.

2. Quote the original message, and then include a notation to indicate it's a retweet, along with credit to the original writer. Common notations include RT for *retweeting;* MT for *modified tweet;* and via, to say that a link or idea came from *@TheirUsername.* HT, for *hat tip,* works like via.

A decent approach is to use the Retweet button when you want to pass along a message verbatim and to quote a message when you want to comment on or change it. **But there are tradeoffs to each approach,** and we discuss them in the next pages.

twitter tip

There are two ways to tell that you're reading something one of your followees passed along using the Retweet button. Your first clue is when you see an incoming message written by someone you don't follow. Your second clue is the Retweet icon—two arrows chasing each other, followed by the name of the person you *do* follow who retweeted the message. Here, Harry Allen has retweeted SLAMJamz Records.

Retweet clearly and classily:
Part 3—use the Retweet button

Back in the day, you could retweet somebody only by cutting and pasting the original message and then typing in all the extra info. Tedious. So when Twitter added the Retweet button in fall 2009—which reduced retweeting to a single click—people were pleased. But **passing along posts with the Retweet button has some drawbacks.**

The good news is that the Retweet button makes your life easy. You just mouse over a tweet, and then click the Retweet link that appears. Twitter passes the message along to your followers verbatim, and it looks like it came from the original writer (as shown on the previous page). You don't have to cut characters or add anything in. Twitter even keeps track of the messages you post with the Retweet button and those you've written that others have retweeted using this method. Just look under the Retweets tab.

The bad news is that you can't comment on the posts or edit them in any way, and not everyone sees the messages you pass along with the button. Who wouldn't see the retweets? Well, messages retweeted with the button don't show up in lists (so anyone who, for instance, pays attention primarily to a "Friends and Family" list, as described in Chapter 2, would miss them). The messages don't show up in Facebook if you use the cross-posting app described in Chapter 5. And people can turn off the button-fed Retweets. (To turn off somebody else's retweets, head to their account page, find the Following button, and click the Retweet icon to the right, shown here.)

Call us new-media traditionalists, but given the tradeoffs, we suggest you hit the Retweet button sparingly and instead get in the habit of using the old-school quoting methods described on the next page.

@MHarrisPerry
Melissa Harris-Perry

RT @dosomething: 5 Things to Do on Labor Day (that Actually Have to Do with Labor) dsorg.us/qgD23D #laborday

11 hours ago via Flipboard ☆ Favorite ⇄ Retweet ↩ Reply

@naypinya
Peter Brantley

MT @michaelzimmer: Seattle Public Library forced to close for a week due to budget cuts. [...]: spl.org

1 Sep via TweetDeck ☆ Favorite ⇄ Retweet ↩ Reply

@timoreilly
Tim O'Reilly ✔

via @psaffo in email: LA Times on Upgrading from a cardboard box for the homeless. http://snurl.com/7rjt7 Neat!

10 Dec 08 via twhirl ☆ Favorite ⇄ Retweet ↩ Reply

@baratunde
Baratunde ✔

an online application that helps people visualize, plan for and reach their dreams bit.ly/mXd165 h/t @priyaparker #Dreamcatcher

1 hour ago via bitly ☆ Favorite ⇄ Retweet ↩ Reply

Retweet clearly and classily: Part 4—quote a tweet

Twitter's Retweet button lets you pass things along without much thought, which explains both its charm and its dark side. When you use it, you may have amplified something of value, but it might have been even more valuable if you'd taken the time to **add a comment, or put your own spin on it and say why you found the link valuable.** (Of course, you'd still want to give credit for the original link.) In addition, for the reasons described on the previous page, not everyone will see the retweet, reducing its impact.

Fortunately, you can easily quote a tweet instead of using the Retweet button; all four examples here are quotes. In fact, most, if not all, third-party clients give you an option to quote instead of retweet (sometimes they call it something like "original-style retweet"). Quoting is, frankly, a missing feature in Twitter, and if you're using their site or programs, you have to cut and paste to quote an existing tweet. A small hassle for a significant payoff.

Here are three good options for quoting a tweet:

1. RT, which stands for *retweet or retweeting.* You start with *RT @Username*, and then follow with the original post (the username is that of the original writer). If you want to comment on the tweet, it's most common to do so *before* the RT, shown on the next pages.

2. MT, which stands for *modified tweet.* Though less common, this is a good choice if you want to include the guts of the original tweet but change or remove a significant point.

3. Via, which describes from whom you got the info, or HT, which stands for *hat tip.* In this case, you can rewrite the whole thing and still give credit. It's also handy for crediting somebody who passed along a link outside Twitter.

@pourmecoffee
pourmecoffee

Tomorrow is Labor Day, when we briefly pause from demonizing unions to enjoy mattress sales in their honor.

4 Sep via TweetDeck ☆ Favorite ⇆ Retweet ↩ Reply

@jennydeluxe
Jenna Wortham ✔

you know you live in New York when you have to duck into the bodega next door for help zipping up your dress and it's TOTALLY COOL

12 Aug via web ☆ Favorite ⇆ Retweet ↩ Reply

@ftrain
Paul Ford

Rather than "obese" I prefer the phrase "too big to fail."

24 Jun via web ☆ Favorite ⇆ Retweet ↩ Reply

@jimog
Jim O'Grady

WNYC massively covers storm when all it need do is RT @lizarnold: Rain-saturated skinny jeans have left my legs an awesome shade of Smurf.

1 Dec via web ☆ Favorite ⇆ Undo Retweet ↩ Reply

What to retweet

Wondering what to retweet? Here are a few standbys:

1. How-tos and instructional stories or videos.

2. News, especially breaking news if you know it's accurate.

3. Warnings, like a scam or virus that's circulating (again check for accuracy).

4. Freebies and contests.

Those are all pretty easy to figure out. But **Twitter is also a great medium for wit, and it's really worth retweeting a funny comment or unique turn of phrase.** We've shown a few of our retweetable recent favorites here.

twitter tip

To have your tweets spread farther, include the phrase "Please retweet" or "Please RT." Researcher Dan Zarrella (@danzarrella) has found that the first phrase generates a *lot* more retweeting and the second phrase a bit more. His post: http://bit.ly/spread-RTs.

@goodappetite
melissa clark

Thanks for the great post Dianne! RT
@diannej: Melissa Clark Works Her Tail
Off and Says You Should Too. New post
bit.ly/qhBCMO

28 Sep via TweetDeck ☆ Favorite ⇋ Retweet ↰ Reply

@carlmalamud
Carl Malamud

RT @edadams: US has too few lawyers &
they're paid too much, study finds.
economist.com/node/21528280?... //
study at least 50% accurate

1 hour ago via TweetDeck ☆ Favorite ⇋ Retweet ↰ Reply

Troubleshoot your retweets

To help you **retweet with confidence,** here's our FAQ for RTs.

1. What if adding the retweeting info bumps me over 140 characters? It's OK to edit down or rewrite a message. If you change it substantially, consider using the MT signifier (instead of RT) or use via or HT, described a couple of pages back.

2. What if I want to add my own comment? No prob, people do it all the time. It's increasingly common to put the comment before the RT or MT, because it's much easier for everyone else to decipher which part is the retweet and which part is the comment. But if you want to comment afterward, just use some punctuation—a couple of slashes, a bar, some less-than symbols—to set off your comment. We show both approaches here.

3. Can I change the URL to make it shorter or to track it? Yup. With tools like Topsy, described in Chapter 2, people can see all the reposts of their links.

4. When I cut and paste or quote a tweet, sometimes the link included appears but no longer links anywhere. What's up with that? Long story short: dueling URL shorteners mean that sometimes, links break during a cut-and-paste maneuver. You can solve the problem by copying in the URL from the target site rather than from the original tweet. Or you can decide not to worry it too much; people who really want to reach the site can paste the link into their browsers.

5. If the list of people who retweeted is getting too long, can I lop off some of them? Yes. But try to give credit to the original poster. Otherwise, you're at risk for misattributing a comment or post—which is a common problem on Twitter.

@zephoria
danah boyd

Anyone have a favorite place to stay in Barcelona? I'm sick of generic hotels. I want a place that feels like I live there. #icwsm

10 May via web ☆ Favorite ⇄ Retweet ↩ Reply

@zephoria
danah boyd

Going to #icwsm? Here are the Barcelona hotel/housing recs that lovely Twitter people suggested: http://bit.ly/jNdJDd

11 May via web ☆ Favorite ⇄ Retweet ↩ Reply

Ask questions

Who's the best flat-top barber in San Francisco?

I'm from NY. Will my iPhone incur roaming charges in Bermuda?

What kind of wine goes with tofu parmesan?

Twitter is a Q&A machine. Here's how you get in on the action: ask a question. People like to help, and Twitter lets them do so by offering just a sentence or two. You won't always get answers, but a lot of the time you will (even if you have just a handful of followers). People on Twitter are delighted to contribute their knowledge.

If you want a more formal process, or if you'd like to reach beyond your own followers, consider **TweetBrain** (http://tweetbrain.com), a Twitter-powered Q&A service.

twitter tip

To be a really good Twitter citizen, don't just ask questions, repost the best answers, too. As you can see here, closing the loop isn't hard, and it makes Twitter more valuable for everyone.

mrgan Neven Mrgan
Parents of twitter: can you recommend a cute toy chest? Bonus points if it doubles
as a bench. Thanks!
16 Aug

in reply to @mrgan ↑

@marcprecipice
Marc Hedlund

@mrgan I've had my eye on this one for a
while: etsy.com/listing/597464... Spendy,
though.

16 Aug via Twitter for Mac

SarahM Sarah Milstein
Is there a light, foldable shopping cart that's great for greenmarketing, followed by
train ride home? I need, like, a stroller for veggies.
20 Aug

in reply to @SarahM ↑

@tamyho
tam ho

@SarahM - not sure if this is quite what
you're looking forl:
opensky.com/doriegreenspan...

20 Aug via web   ☆ Favorite ⇄ Retweet ↩ Reply

Answer questions

The people you follow on Twitter may wonder where to find the best espresso in Rome, or how to train their cats from jumping up on the counters or whether PowerPoint slides can be displayed in portrait orientation. If you know the answers, don't hesitate to respond with a friendly @reply.

If you want to amp up your answering, keep an eye on Twitter search for keywords in questions you might be able to answer. (As we explain in Chapter 2, Twitter's advanced search lets you look for people asking questions.) For instance, if you're a motorcycle mechanic, you might run searches for questions containing "Harley," "Yamaha" and perhaps "broken." Though you have to use judgment about approaching strangers, **providing good info on Twitter can help you develop a positive reputation.**

twitter tip

If you run a local business and you're looking for work, use Twitter's advanced search to find people in your area asking questions you might be able to answer. Of course, be wary of appearing to stalk people, and follow the prudent business practices outlined in Chapter 6.

As a poller...I need to find a way to work this like my next presentation...Sarah Palin: "Polls are for Strippers" http://ow.ly/6kUBk

4 Sep

 RepsLuvGov Curtis Below

@SarahM @mattcutts Wondering the same thing. Looks like it is still there, but you need to look at the preview page seroundtable.com/google-similar...

4 Sep ☆ Favorite ⇄ Retweet ↩ Reply

 RepsLuvGov Curtis Below

@markos It's time to dispense with the "small gov't" Rep meme.

close ✕

 SarahM Sarah Milstein

What happened to the "Similar" link in Google results?(!) Looks like it's gone...so is there a way to get that info now? /cc @mattcutts

1 Sep

in reply to ↑

@RepsLuvGov
Curtis Below

@SarahM @mattcutts Wondering the same thing. Looks like it is still there, but you need to look at the preview page seroundtable.com/google-similar...

4 Sep via web

☆ Favorite ⇄ Retweet ↩ Reply

Send smart @replies

We see @replies like these every day:

"I hope not."

"She's my favorite!"

"Aren't we all?"

"Don't waste your money or time reading the trash he peddles!"

"Wow."

Seem meaningless to you without context? Seems that way to us, too, and these are actual @replies we've received.

When you respond to a tweet, you can make things clearer by using the Twitter Reply link (described earlier in this chapter) instead of typing in @*Username*. The beauty of the Reply link is that it *threads* your conversation, and when you click a tweet in your timeline, a box opens to the right, showing your exchange. You can tell a tweet is part of a thread by the appearance of the tiny conversation balloon icon, shown here.

Of course, you can also ensure that your co-conversationalists know what you're talking about by sending @replies that provide a touch of context.

@RepsLuvGov
Curtis Below

@PaulBegala Enjoyed your "I <3 Gov't" story, esp the last line: thedailybeast.com/newsweek/2011/.... Reps really do love gov't: republicanslovegovernment.com

16 Sep via web ☆ Favorite ⏄ Retweet ↰ Reply

@BerginoBaseball
Jay Goldberg

@SamRyanSports Always enjoy your work. Invite to Clubhouse event on 9/24 - The Baseball Art of James Fiorentino. bit.ly/nNOxEO

18 Sep via web ☆ Favorite ⏄ Retweet ↰ Reply
from Manhattan, NY

@digiphile
Alex Howard

Washington, D.C. publishes its first #digitaldivide strategy http://bit.ly /hX9Evp #gov20 #opengov /cc @PeterShankman

9 Dec via TweetDeck ☆ Favorite ⏄ Retweet ↰ Reply

@sarahm check us out for #thetwitterbook. bio searches, user comparisons, social graph tracking, follower segmentation

15 Sep via web ☆ Favorite ⏄ Retweet ↰ Reply

@SarahM thanks for checking us out. any questions? ;) (we did upgrade your acct btw.)

15 Sep via TweetDeck ☆ Favorite ⏄ Retweet ↰ Reply
from Portland, OR

SarahM Sarah Milstein
No questions, thanks
15 Sep
in reply to @SarahM

@SarahM super... by the way, here's who you, @timoreilly and @sarahpalinusa have in common in terms of follows wonk.ly/8LPt

15 Sep via TweetDeck ☆ Favorite ⏄ Retweet ↰ Reply
from Portland, OR

Get attention gracefully

As you get comfortable tweeting, you might well be tempted to **reach out to prominent people and journalists on Twitter** in order to draw attention to your own writing, projects, events and products. Twitter can be a good medium for contacting people you wouldn't otherwise have access to, but there's fine line between friendly outreach and stalking. Here are a few tips for garnering positive attention. At the end of this chapter, we describe spam on Twitter, which is well worth understanding *before* you alienate people.

1. Do think about building relationships rather than randomly approaching people who might—or might not—be interested in your work. On Twitter, relationships can be fairly lightweight, but they usually involve following the person of interest, thoughtfully retweeting them, answering their questions, and occasionally suggesting *other* people's work that may be of interest to them. As you get to know somebody, cc'ing them on a tweet of possible interest is an option, as Alex Howard (@digiphile) does here.

2. Do demonstrate that you're familiar with the person's work. When you post links to their stuff, include a well-crafted editorial comment and their @username.

3. When you invite them to look at your stuff, be gracious and low key. See how Jay Goldberg (@BerginoBaseball) and Curtis Below (@RepsLuvGov) do that here?

4. Don't be overly aggressive while pretending to be helpful. Here, you can see that a company has @messaged Sarah three times rapidly after somebody else publicly suggested she look into them, and she'd already replied that she would. She didn't ask for the upgrade, by the way, nor did she want it; ditto the Sarah Palin info.

@mkapor
Mitch Kapor

Nothing in my tweet stream except
Superbowl chatter, more about ads than
the game. No offense, but wish there were
a mute button.

6 Feb via web ☆ Favorite ⇄ Retweet ↩ Reply

@ericries
Eric Ries

Want to temporarily mute the #sllconf
firehose? RT @DarlasRock: How To
Temporarily Silence Followers in Twitter
http://ericri.es/lx6fmg

23 May via TweetDeck ☆ Favorite ⇄ Retweet ↩ Reply

@heymarci
marci alboher ✓

Tks @dawnbugni! Several ways to mute
folks during chats: http://is.gd/Zg9ljf &
http://is.gd/rfU2kb (More, Google
"Muting Tweets")

26 Jul via HootSuite ☆ Favorite ⇄ Retweet ↩ Reply

Tweet often...but not too often

Twitter novitiates almost always wonder, "How often should I tweet?" (Actually, Twitter pros wonder this, too.) Like most things in Twitter, there is no Right Answer.

When we published the first edition of this book, **there was an average number of tweets per day among all users:** 4.22. We haven't been able to get new data, but that number is still a good guide. If you want to build relationships and a positive reputation on Twitter, you should post at least a few times a week and perhaps a few times a day.

That said, many of the most popular people on Twitter post a couple of dozen times a day, and research has shown that more tweets lead to more followers. The lesson? Start with whatever feels right, then tweak it to see what works for you. **HowOftenDoYouTweet** (http://howoftendoyoutweet.com) will show you your daily average.

twitter tip

If you're an average poster, and you occasionally tweet up a storm (say when you're attending a conference, as we discuss in Chapter 4), you should expect some of your followers to be pleased and others to be appalled by the sudden uptick. In the examples here, you can see some thoughts on muting, plus links to how-tos.

cvmartinez Chris Martinez
#usopen Momentum shift. Wozniacki looks like she'll take 2nd set. #latenightahead
26 seconds ago

peteminn Peter Jack
Wow. Wozniacki is right back in this match. I thought she was done for. **#usopen**
25 seconds ago

justinmgibson Justin M. Gibson
#Kuznetsova and #Wozniacki are balling out at the **#USOpen**... Winner has chance to lose to @serenawilliams in semis
20 seconds ago

LSUCait Caitilin
Wozniacki and Kuznetsova make for great entertainment!! Excellent match-up. **#usopen**
28 seconds ago

Anti_Intellect Educator

Three cool hashtag tricks

In Chapter 1, we describe hashtags, which let people group messages by category—making them an important element of conversations on Twitter. Once you get the hang of the idea, **you can adapt it for lots of purposes.** Here are a few of our favorite uses:

1. Group chat. Got a discussion you want to hold among a bunch of people who aren't in the same place? Designate a hashtag and a particular hour or so for the chat. Put the word out to the appropriate community. Use a tool like **TweetGrid** (http://tweetgrid.com) or **TweetChat** (http://tweetchat.com) to stay on top of the conversation and moderate it. (Note that hashtags are not case sensitive.)

To find existing chats—or to list a new one—check out the amazing, editable Google doc Meryl K. Evans has created, where people add Twitter chats and their relevant info. She links to it from her blog: http://bit.ly/twitterchats.

2. Collect ideas. Ask a question on Twitter ("What are your favorite new romance novels?") and give a hashtag people can use to share their answers (#romancenov).

3. Share an experience. Loving an American Idol performance? Not so thrilled with Hollywood's latest blockbuster? Just felt a tremble? Use a hashtag to weigh in (#AmericanIdol, #007, #earthquake). For events like these, in which lots of people participate, there's almost certain to be an existing hashtag. Check Twitter search.

☐ ▼	Remove label	Spam	Delete	⊕ ⊖	Move to ▼	Labels ▼	More ▼	C		1 - 50 of 36501	◄ ►

☐ ☆ Twitter		Twitter	Bert (@Bdert) is now following you on Twitter! - Twitter Bert @E	9:41 pm
☐ ☆ Twitter	»	Twitter	Testimonial Monkey (@TMonkey_UK) is now following you on	7:12 pm
☐ ☆ Twitter		Twitter	Santosha Space (@santoshaspace) is now following you on Tv	6:46 pm
☐ ☆ Twitter		Twitter	Randy Hellman (@rthellman) has sent you a direct message or	4:32 pm
☐ ☆ Twitter	»	Twitter	Anil Dash (@anildash) favorited one of your Tweets! - Twitter Ar	4:15 pm
☐ ☆ Twitter	»	Twitter	nmsanchez (@nmsanchez) replied to one of your Tweets! - Twi	4:14 pm
☐ ☆ Twitter		Twitter	LE ZHANG (@happygatto) is now following you on Twitter! - Tw	3:15 pm
☐ ☆ Twitter	»	Twitter	Clearwater Chamber (@ClearwaterArea) replied to one of you	1:58 pm
☐ ☆ Twitter (2)	»	Twitter	Billy Stubblebine (@BillyAwesome) replied to one of your Twe	1:56 pm
☐ ☆ Twitter	»	Twitter	Billy Stubblebine (@BillyAwesome) mentioned you on Twitter!	1:32 pm
☐ ☆ Twitter		Twitter	uğur ipek (@Dehumanizati0n) is now following you on Twitter!	1:30 pm
☐ ☆ Twitter		Twitter	saboor (@sab_eminem) is now following you on Twitter! - Twitt	11:48 am
☐ ☆ Twitter		Twitter	LinkLocal_Schaumburg (@SchaumburgLink) is now following	7:15 am
☐ ☆ Twitter	»	Twitter	Robert Gerald (@robgerald) is now following you on Twitter! -	5:36 am

Know your followers

When you first sign up for Twitter, it's set to send you an email every time somebody new follows you. If you don't like the interruption, create an email folder and filter for the messages so that they can pile up without bothering you.

Every now and then, you can peek at the list, which will look like the one we've shown here, and **see who you might want to follow back or say hello to.**

Even with this email record, it doesn't take long to lose track of who's following you and even who you're following. These tools provide **insight into your network.**

1. If you're wondering whether an account follows you, **DoesFollow** (http://doesfollow.com) will let you check easily.

2. To see all your followees, fans (i.e., followers) and friends (mutual followers), try **FriendOrFollow** (http://friendorfollow.com).

twitter tip

If you decide you don't want email messages from Twitter when you get new followers, you can turn them off. Head to the upper-right corner of your account page, click the arrow next to your name, and then go to Settings → Notifications.

@simonpegg
Simon Pegg ✓

Love it when people I don't know inform me they are unfollowing. Like a stranger coming up to you in a pub and saying "Right, I'm leaving!"

8 Sep via TweetDeck ☆ Unfavorite ⇄ Retweet ↩ Reply

Unfollow graciously

There's no rule saying that once you follow somebody, you have to follow them forever. In fact, one of the useful things about Twitter is that **you can follow somebody for a while, get a sense of their universe, and then unfollow** in order to tune into somebody else for a bit.

Twitter itself doesn't tell somebody when you unfollow her, and in most cases, the person won't know. That said, there are third-party applications that will alert people when they've been unfollowed, so some Twitterers do know. Either way, should you tell them why you're unfollowing? Nah. Chances are, you're leaving the account for the very reasons other people love it.

To unfollow somebody, head to her account page. Under her picture, simply click the "Following" button.

By the way, we can't recommend signing up for services that send you unfollow notices. First, they lend to obsessing about popularity. Second, they purport to tell you when people unfollow you after a certain tweet, but they rarely, if ever, show that data accurately. And even if they did, you still wouldn't know *why* somebody unfollowed. We suggest cultivating good relationships where you can and not worrying about the rest.

Don't auto-DM (for crying out loud)

Imagine you're at a conference chatting with a few people before the next session starts. Suddenly, somebody shouts across the room, "Nice to meet you! You can learn more about me and my consulting service at www.iampushy.com." From another corner of the room you hear, "Thanks for being in the same room! Can't wait to get to know you!"

You're likely to consider that sort of overture intrusive. And chances are, it's not going to lead to a meaningful exchange.

Auto-DMs—which are generic direct messages some people send when you follow them—work the same way: they're impersonal, disruptive and almost never spark a good conversation. In fact, when you think about them that way, **they sound a lot like spam—which is what they are.**

Take a look at the three examples here: can you imagine the recipient being delighted to get them? (She wasn't.)

If you must acknowledge a new follower, do a little research, figure out what you have in common and send a personal message.

@randomdeanna
Deanna Zandt

.@gbedard1 I don't have a relationship to you or your work, so randomly tweeting me isn't going to make me click your link

9 Sep via Twitter for Android   ☆ Unfavorite ⇄ Retweet ↩ Reply

@randomdeanna
Deanna Zandt

.@gbedard1 when I check out who you are, I see you're randomly tweeting a lot of ppl, so now you kinda look like a spammer. oh noes!

9 Sep via Twitter for Android   ☆ Unfavorite ⇄ Retweet ↩ Reply

@randomdeanna
Deanna Zandt

.@gbedard1 Twitter isn't a shortcut to popularity. It's a means to build relationships.

9 Sep via Twitter for Android   ☆ Unfavorite ⇄ Retweet ↩ Reply

@randomdeanna
Deanna Zandt

.@gbedard1 So start getting to know the ppl whose attention you want, and let them get to know you. *Then* pitch them shamelessly. :) /end

9 Sep via Twitter for Android   ☆ Unfavorite ⇄ Retweet ↩ Reply

Don't spam anyone

Here's an important point to remember: Twitter is an opt-in medium, which means that **if you're obnoxious or even a little bit spammy, people will unfollow you** or they'll choose not to follow you in the first place. (They can also block you and suggest that you get kicked off Twitter, which we talk about on the next page.) On Twitter, spam is self-defeating.

As we discuss on the previous page, auto-DMs are a form of spam. A few other forms of tweeting are also spam, and you should avoid all of them.

This ought to go without saying, but if you're DMing people with the goal of selling something, you're committing spam. Don't kid yourself into thinking that a discount or a freebie is a legit message, either. Rule of thumb: if you're tempted to DM a bunch of people you don't know, you're very likely about to become a spammer.

Ditto @messages. If you're sending @messages to people who don't know you, and your notes aren't in response to something they've said or done, or a question or a comment related to their expertise, you'll probably be perceived as a spammer. Here, social media strategist Deanna Zandt (@randomdeanna) explains to a potential spammer how these messages are perceived.

Finally, as in email, if your iffy messages contain links, other people are more likely to believe they're spam.

@timoreilly, sign up for Klout and see how we compare! klout.com/timoreilly?n=t...

1 Sep via Tweet Button ☆ Favorite ⇄ Retweet ↩ Reply

Daily Blog News is out! bit.ly/jgJtm3 ▸ Top stories today via @cayzer @sarahm

16 Sep via Paper.li ☆ Favorite ⇄ Retweet ↩ Reply

 @Borthwick
John Borthwick

testing new #socialsearch to find all links my friends posted to twitter. Join me at social-search.com

19 Sep via folkd.com ☆ Favorite ⇄ Retweet ↩ Reply

 @Borthwick
John Borthwick

Hate it when services auto-tweet. -1 for social search

1 hour ago via TweetDeck ☆ Favorite ⇄ Retweet ↩ Reply

Don't let third-party apps spam (or tweet) on your behalf

We have a real distaste for apps that tweet on your behalf, particularly those that include @mentions, **without adding any value for your followers.** Summify, Klout, Paper.li, Utopic.me—we're looking at you. For instance, what does anyone (other than perhaps Klout and Paper.li) gain from the first two messages shown here?

Presumably the idea is that the people mentioned in these tweets will be pleased to see themselves noted, and you will endear yourself to them with the @mention. We can tell you, however, on good authority, that the people mentioned in these tweets are not at all pleased. Moreover, nobody else wants to read these posts. Why? Because they amount to spam, giving no contextual information and requiring click-throughs to the third-party sites that *then* direct people to the real content. Of course, Twitter has a well-established system for pointing your followers to great stuff and giving credit to the people who helped you discover it: retweets, which we discussed in depth earlier in this chapter.

Another set of services tweet ads for themselves, via your account, when you use them (take a look at the third message here, which John Borthwick [@Borthwick] unwittingly sent by using Social-Search.com). If you think a service is really great, and you want other people to know about it, tweet in your own words.

To avoid spamming people via third-party apps, simply be careful when you're clicking around them, and skip, opt out or uncheck any choice to tweet about the app.

There are some apps from which you might want to tweet, like Foursquare. In Chapter 5, we discuss how to do so gracefully.

hey guys!!!!!!!! i found a really cool blog which is interesting and helpful,just check it out and just post me ur opinion http://ping ......

5:45 AM Mar 24th from Ping.fm

hey i found a ultra cool blog,check this out,it will help you really, http://   .blogspot...

1:04 AM Mar 24th from web

@nnphoto Reading My friend   y's new blog...http://   .blogspot... really ultra kool!

12:12 PM Mar 12th from web in reply to nnphoto

@feliciaday Reading My friend   y's new blog...http://   .blogspot... really ultra kool!

12:11 PM Mar 12th from web in reply to feliciaday

@iamdiddy Reading My friend   y's new blog...http://   blogspot... really ultra kool!

12:11 PM Mar 12th from web in reply to iamdiddy

Fight spam

Internet culture expert Clay Shirky (@cshirky) has said that online social systems are, by definition, "stuff that gets spammed." Twitter is no exception.

Twitter spam comes in two primary forms: random @messages and random direct messages. If you receive an @message from somebody you don't know offering a link to a site that "will make you feel better" or a direct message suggesting that your ultimate happiness is just a click away, you've been spammed. Here's how you can fight it:

1. Follow one of Twitter's spam-fighting accounts, @spam or @safety, which give tips on types of spam and reminders on how to report it.

2. Report the spammer. Just head over to the spammer's account page and look to the right of the Follow (or Following) button for the icon of a person. Click that to get a menu that includes "Report *Username* for spam."

3. Unfollow the spammer. If you're following the account, now's a good time to unfollow it. Go to the spammer's account page, and in the upper-left corner, under the picture, click Following.

@zoefinkel
zoe finkel

That last weight loss article was a hack. Is now deleted and password changed.

9 Sep via web ☆ Favorite ⇄ Retweet ↩ Reply

@safety
Safety ✓

Is your account sending DMs/Tweets without yr involvement? Not Skynet; you're phished. Follow these steps: bit.ly/accountamiss.

3 Sep via Twitter for iPhone ☆ Favorite ⇄ Retweet ↩ Reply

@tonystubblebine
Tony Stubblebine

I'M BACK! The worst part about having your account suspended is not being able to tweet about it.

2 Jun via web ☆ Favorite ⇄ Retweet ↩ Reply
from South Beach, San Francisco

Recover fast
if your account is compromised

From time to time, you may see one of your friends tweet out odd messages touting weight loss schemes or exhortations to "Just click here" or other spammy notes. Unless Jenny Craig is your BFF, chances are that your friend's account has been hacked—i.e., compromised by a spammer. Indeed, the same thing could happen to you, and while it's upsetting, **it's easy to recover, and it's well understood on Twitter that this happens occasionally, even to the best of us.**

You'll know your account has been hacked if it's suddenly sending tweets or DMs you didn't create, or if it's creepily following, unfollowing or blocking accounts on it own. (Often, your followers will let you know if they're seeing fishy tweets.) Assuming you can still log into your account, follow the steps below (if you can't log in, and your account has been suspended accidently, follow the directions at http://bit.ly/cant-login; here, Tony Stubblebine [@tonystubblebine] expresses a common frustration with accidental suspensions).

1. Change your password. In the upper-right corner of your account page, click the arrow next to your username → Settings → Password. Bear in mind that when you sign into any third-party apps, you'll have to update your password.

2. Check your third-party applications. Under Settings › Applications, look for any programs you don't recognize and click Revoke Access.

3. Let people know your account was hacked, and you've fixed the problem. Zoe Finkel (@zoefinkel) gives the perfect, simple explanation here.

If you see that a friend's account has recently been hacked, shoot them a quick email or text.

CHAPTER 4 | Share Information and Ideas

Twitter is a terrific place to share information and ideas. But with only 140 characters per message—approximately the length of a news headline—clear communication can be challenging.

In this chapter, we look at some of **the smartest ways people have found to post cool information, achieve clarity and make the most of Twitter's space constraint.**

By the way, if you're interested in using Twitter to network and help you find a job, pay special attention to the ideas in this chapter and the next two. Although the last chapter is about business uses of Twitter, a lot of the concepts apply to any professional.

@jdbookbinder
Judith Bookbinder

2 or more cups of coffee a day may help prevent depression in women: http://ow.ly/6FZE9 I find coffee also helps with Fruit Ninja scores.

🔒 13 hours ago via HootSuite ☆ Unfavorite ↩ Reply

@MarthaStewart
Martha Stewart ✓

The drinks and this salad are at myong in mt kisco new york- a creative dining experience twitpic.com/6kzqyk

 TwitPic   Flag this media

18 hours ago via Twitter for BlackBerry® ☆ Unfavorite ↩ Retweet ↩ Reply

@davidlebovitz
David Lebovitz ✓

The sadness I feel over a good friend moving away is mitigated somewhat by the substantial stash of ziplock bags I'll be inheriting.

11 hours ago via web ☆ Favorite ↩ Retweet ↩ Reply

Be interesting to other people

Twitter routes millions of messages a day about what people are eating for lunch. Not that you shouldn't report on your grilled cheese—or any other details of your day. We're firm believers that exchanging those quotidian snapshots can make people feel more connected to each other.

But do bear in mind that Twitter is an *opt-in* medium. Which means that if you aren't interesting, people will unfollow you or choose not to follow you in the first place.

So before you post a message, take a second to **think about whether there's a more entertaining or informative way to give the update.** Can you poke a little fun at yourself? Make an offbeat observation? Add a link or a picture that helps people understand what you're talking about? (We explain later in this chapter how to include pictures in your tweets.)

@nancyfranklin
Nancy Franklin

People, @BobBalaban is now on twitter. And there are pictures of his daughter's boyfriend's dog. But don't take *my* word for it!

31 minutes ago via web ☆ Favorite ⇄ Retweet ↩ Reply

@acroll
Alistair Croll

wow, @doctorow is really really good at humanizing the privacy debates surrounding big data. #strataconf

20 Sep via Twitter for iPhone ☆ Unfavorite ⇄ Retweet ↩ Reply

@sree
Sree Sreenivasan

.@ChristieM & team making doc about web & technology are looking for YOUR input (not money!) to finish it: bit.ly/oUGYxX

20 Sep via SocialFlow ☆ Favorite ⇄ Retweet ↩ Reply

@profblmkelley
Blair LM Kelley

.@milfinainteasy I didn't see the letter as a denunciation. I do think it's important to have a broad conversation about the idea.

28 Sep via Echofon ☆ Favorite ⇄ Retweet ↩ Reply

Make sure your messages get seen

Twitter is set to show you only the @messages between people you're following. For example, if you're following Jane but not Joe, you won't see any @messages between Jane and Joe. Conversely, if you're following both Jane and Pete, you'll see the @messages between them.

Hardly anyone is aware of this setting, but it's hugely important. Because it means that when you start a message with the @ symbol, the vast majority of people won't see it. Which may be fine by you if you're sending somebody an @reply, but it's probably the opposite of what you want if you're trying to *refer* to somebody.

For instance, imagine you're followed by 3,500 people, ten of whom are also following Kermit the Frog. When you tweet, "@kermie's new book is amazing; get a copy at http://bit.ly/kerm," only the ten people following both of you will see your message. Which is almost certainly not your intention.

The solution is easy: unless you're sending an @message, don't start your posts with the @ symbol. Instead, rewrite your sentence, or start with something like, "Wow," "Cool," "This just in." Alternatively, put a period or other punctuation before the username to start your tweet. In our bottom two examples here, both start with a period. Sree Sreenivasan (@sree) uses it because he's referring to @ChristineM rather than talking to her. Blair Kelley (@profblmkelley) begins with a period because she both wants to respond to @milfinainteasy, *and* she wants everyone else to see her reply.

@andrewsavikas
Andrew Savikas

"Literally everything is wrong with this pie chart" http://j.mp/dqxqcP (via @newsycombinator)

13 Sep via Echofon   ☆ Unfavorite ⇄ Retweet ↩ Reply

@finiteattention
Chris Atherton

Ever wanted to know which Pantone colour the best selling bananas have? And other sales tricks. is.gd/SZ92pZ /via @tkb

19 hours ago via Twitter for iPhone   ☆ Favorite ⇄ Retweet ↩ Reply

@cookingforgeeks
Jeff Potter

In case you missed it: how to start a fire using Doritos: lifehac.kr/pkNGRA

7 hours ago via TweetDeck   ☆ Favorite ⇄ Retweet ↩

@nickbilton
Nick Bilton ✔

The Rise of the Zuckerverb: The New Language of Facebook: bit.ly/rsnhTN (Interesting piece by @bgzimmer)

30 Sep via Twitter for Mac   ☆ Favorite ⇄ Retweet ↩ Reply

Link to interesting stuff around the web

Twitter asks, "What's happening?" If you're reading, watching, hearing, cooking and playing great stuff, Twitter is the perfect way to share links to those things.

In addition to **helping other people find cool stuff, there's a self-interested good reason to link liberally:** your messages that contain well-described, cool links are most likely to be retweeted. Plus, if you regularly share great links on a topic, people will come to see you as a resource, which can boost your professional reputation.

From the examples here, you can see that 140 characters give plenty of space to create a *compelling* pointer to a web page and include a shortened URL (we discuss URL shorteners in Chapters 1 and 6). Note that sometimes, quoting a story, rather than describing it, can be an excellent teaser. Also, thoughtful editorial comments on the stuff you link to are welcome.

twitter tip

Here, Nick Bilton (@nickbilton) notes that @bgzimmer wrote the post he links to. That's smart, not only because it gives credit publicly, but also because it lets the author (who may well be keeping an eye on his @mentions) know you like his stuff. And that may lead to a new follower. Often, you need to Google for somebody's Twitter handle, but it's well worth taking the time to include it.

@ebertchicago
Roger Ebert ✔

A great one on Netflix Instant for you. "Bill Cunningham New York." Watch five minutes and you love him. My review: bit.ly/iM60HK

24 Sep via SocialOomph ☆ Favorite ⇄ Retweet ↩ Reply

@101Cookbooks
101 Cookbooks

Snapshots from my visit to W. Virginia + the Brown Butter Rosemary Walnuts I packed for the flight: bit.ly/pr4i5X

20 Sep via web ☆ Unfavorite ⇄ Retweet ↩ Reply

@fredwilson
Fred Wilson

i'm taking heat in the comments for this post http://bit.ly/96C91 and some of it well deserved and well said. a much needed discussion

24 Mar 09 via Power Twitter ☆ Favorite ⇄ Retweet ↩ Reply

@bjfogg
BJ Fogg

How can I help you? Here's a new way: bit.ly/askbjfogg

38 minutes ago via web ☆ Favorite ⇄ Retweet ↩ Reply

Link appealingly to your blog or site

People and organizations around the web report that tweeting links to their own sites can drive a lot of traffic. Indeed, Twitter has become the top referrer for a lot of sites.

The key to generating click-throughs is writing an appealing little introduction to the post or page you're linking to. Think of it as a headline tailored for your Twitter audience, and—like those we've shown here—consider inviting people to participate.

Do bear in mind that simply posting a feed of headlines from your blog or site can drive people away. Instead, when you post a link, contextualize it for your followers.

Finally, as we mentioned back in Chapter 2, don't forget to leave enough room in your post for people to retweet your message easily.

twitter tip

Want your recent tweets to show up on your blog or site, along with a link to follow you? Twitter has widgets you can use: http://twitter.com/widgets.

@timoreilly
Tim O'Reilly

This @wsj article hints at some of the complex economics that keep #ebook prices high. My take: bit.ly/ovmWoX

13 Sep via Seesmic   ☆ Unfavorite ⇄ Retweet ↰ Reply

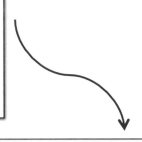

 Google+   🏠 🖼 ⑨ 🔗 ⋈   Search Google+

 Tim O'Reilly · Sep 13, 2011 · Public

This @wsj article hints at some of the complex economics that keep ebook prices high. While it's true that ebooks don't have as much manufacturing cost associated with them, the manufacturing cost has always been a surprisingly small part of the overall cost of a book, except in the case of massively-hyped books that fail to live up to expectations. For example, for O'Reilly books in the heyday of print publishing, our manufacturing costs were always in the 15-16% of net sales range (i.e. roughly 8% of list price.)

Now that print runs are getting smaller, manufacturing costs actually go up (because printing costs go down with volume). So a book whose sales are 50% print and 50% ebook might actually have higher manufacturing costs than when the book was p-only.

Meanwhile, the fixed costs of bringing a book to market are fairly high, at least for traditional publishers. Those costs have to be spread across all revenue sources for the book - both p- and e-.

As the attached WSJ article hints, there is downward pricing pressure from new low-cost self-publishers even though Amazon is no longer able to drive prices down by selling below cost.

Meanwhile, in some cases lower prices drive much higher volumes, but this isn't always the case.

Net-net: expect publishers to experiment a lot with prices, to see what the tradeoffs are. In the end, though, it's important to realize that most publishers aren't trying to gouge customers with a product that is somehow "free" to them. They are trying to stay afloat by recouping the cost of developing their product plus a reasonable profit.

Use the hub-and-spoke model to your advantage

Twitter! Facebook! Google+! Blogs! YouTube! Tumblr! Flickr! Foursquare! **There are a lot of social media sites out there competing not just for your eyeballs but for your fingertips,** enjoining you to create more stuff to share with the world. We've listed just a few, and by the time you're reading this book, there will no doubt be additional services that other people think you should to try.

Here's one way to keep up: pick one, maybe two, of the sites for your primary activity, and consider those your hub. Think of the others as spokes where you post stuff, and then use your hub to send people down the spokes, and vice versa.

For instance, Tim is, of course, quite active on Twitter. But the 140-character limit doesn't allow for deeper conversations. So lately, he's been using Google+ to post more substantive commentary. Then he links to it from Twitter, as you can see here. Another advantage of this approach is that Google+ lets others share longer responses to his post.

We've seen people create successful hubs out of most of the sites mentioned above, and then use Twitter to feed into them. We've also seen (and done) the opposite. Bear in mind that this is different from cross-posting (discussed in Chapter 5), where you post the same thing to more than one social site.

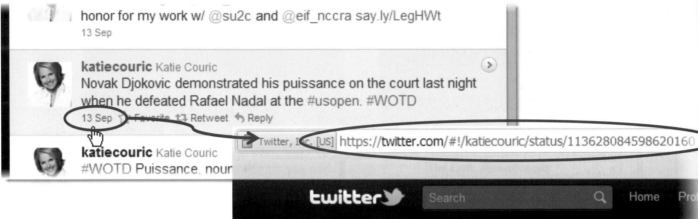

honor for my work w/ @su2c and @eif_nccra say.ly/LegHWt
13 Sep

katiecouric Katie Couric
Novak Djokovic demonstrated his puissance on the court last night
when he defeated Rafael Nadal at the #usopen. #WOTD
13 Sep ☆ Favorite ⇄ Retweet ↩ Reply

katiecouric Katie Couric
#WOTD Puissance, noun

Twitter, Inc. [US] https://twitter.com/#!/katiecouric/status/113628084598620160

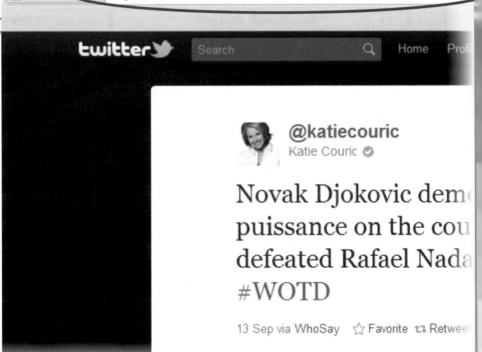

twitter 🐦   Search   🔍   Home   Prof

@**katiecouric**
Katie Couric ✔

Novak Djokovic dem
puissance on the cou
defeated Rafael Nada
#WOTD

13 Sep via WhoSay   ☆ Favorite   ⇄ Retweet

Link to a tweet

Every now and then, you see **a tweet so poignant, smart or funny, you want to send it around** to other people. But how do you link to an individual tweet?

Easy. When you see a tweet either in your incoming timeline or on somebody else's account page, it'll always include the time it was posted. That time stamp is actually a link to the permanent URL for an individual message. Click the time stamp link to open a page with that single message. (Katie Couric [@katiecouric], shown here, has a word-of-the-day [#WOTD] series going. Her vocabulary is better than network television would have you think.)

Note that in Chapter 2, we give you tips on finding old tweets.

When you want to link to a series of related tweets, try **Storify** (http://storify.com), which lets you create a single, readable post out of tweets, photos, video and text.

twitter tip

See how there's a blue checkmark next to Couric's name? That means her account has been *verified*, Twitter's process for confirming that accounts actually belong to well-known people. Conversely, there's a whole world of parody accounts, including @MayorEmanuel, @FakeAPStylebook, @DarthVader and @BronxZoosCobra.

Peculiar morning. 1. I slept in. 2. I woke up with "Sister Christian" playing in my head.
10 hours ago

danmil Dan Milstein
Some days, being a parent is hard. Other days, you put your twins in hoodies, and your life is crazy cute. yfrog.com/nwb9gvj
10 hours ago ☆ Favorite ⇄ Retweet ↩ Reply

FortGreeneAssn FortGreeneAssn
Portrait of a Changing Neighborhood: Isabel Garcia bit.ly/gSr089

@danmil
Dan Milstein

Some days, being a parent is hard. Other days, you put your twins in hoodies, and your life is crazy cute. yfrog.com/nwb9gvj

YFrog   Flag this media

10 hours ago via Twitterrific
☆ Favorite ⇄ Retweet ↩ Reply

Post pictures

A picture, as you know, is **worth a good deal more than 140 characters.** Indeed, sharing images has become big on Twitter. There are a few ways to do it, all of them easy.

On the Twitter site, when you click the "What's happening?" box, a little camera icon appears below it. Click the camera, and Twitter opens a dialog box to help you find and upload a photo from your drives. The downside with this method is that Twitter doesn't tell you how many people view the pics you tweet. Services like **TwitPic** (http://twitpic.com) and **Yfrog** (http://yfrog.com) do count views, which makes them useful alternatives—and, helpfully, they're baked into third-party clients like Seesmic (see Chapter 2). In addition, photo-sharing sites like **Flickr** (http://flickr.com) usually have a "Share on Twitter" button.

Your phone was practically made for tweeting photos, and all the mobile clients let you share seamlessly. From an iPhone, try **Instagram** (http://instagr.am), for snazzy effects.

twitter tip
As you can see here, photos show up as links, and you have to click the tweet or link to open a box on the right where you can see the pic. Thus, links to pictures really benefit from a snappy description in your tweet. Which link do you click through: "Yesterday in the park" or "Rosie the Rottweiler meets Chico the Chihuahua"?

@baratunde
Baratunde ✓

"just b/c something is publicly accessible doesn't mean people want it to be publicized" - @zephoria #sxsw

13 Mar 10 via web   ☆ Favorite   ♺ Retweet   ↩ Reply

@timoreilly
Tim O'Reilly ✓

"Coal plants kill people, but they only kill a few at a time, which is highly preferred by politicians." @BillGates #wiredbiz

3 May via Seesmic Desktop   ☆ Favorite   ♺ Retweet   ↩ Reply

@dooce
Heather B. Armstrong ✓

About to appear onstage with @CTurlington at Social Good Summit. She is the tall one. @92Y #SocialGood

5 minutes ago via Twitter for iPhone   ☆ Favorite   ♺ Retweet   ↩ Reply

@finiteattention
Chris Atherton

Good morning, all. If anyone's travelling to #TCUK11 from central Oxford this evening and would like to share a cab, please ping me! Ta.

6 hours ago via Twitter for iPhone   ☆ Favorite   ♺ Retweet   ↩ Reply

Live-tweet an event

If you're at a conference or event, Twitter is a **great way to amplify the smart ideas and connect with others.** Just type up the juiciest bits and give credit to the speakers (if possible, use their Twitter handles to increase the likelihood that they'll get proper credit and that they'll see your tweets), or post your request. If the event has a hashtag, include it.

If you're organizing an event, be sure to encourage live-tweeting by *creating and publicizing the hashtag*. The messages people post will help get the word out about your conference, and if enough people tweet, your event may trend on Twitter, particularly in local markets (described in Chapter 2), providing free publicity.

As an organizer, you can take things a step further by projecting tweets from your event on screens around the site; **ParaTweet** is a good tool for this (http://paratweet.com). As a speaker, you can designate somebody to track tweets about your talk and give real-time feedback or hold live Q&A via Twitter.

twitter tip

If you're live-tweeting an event, put the hashtag at the end of your tweets, not the beginning. Makes them *much* easier for other people to read.

@tayari
Tayari Jones

I would like to give a shout out to the travel app on my iPhone. I love you @tripit

7 Jun via TweetDeck ☆ Favorite ⇄ Retweet ↰ Reply

@crystal
crystal

Totally loved An Taigh Osda- if traveling to Scotland, don't miss Islay, & stay here! #thankspaul #farewellislay 4sq.com/ofYylh

@doctorow
Cory Doctorow

Hey, @QantasAirways! We're stranded in Las Vegas with a screwed up Qantas miles ticket & no one will answer the phone at your end - help!

9 Sep via web ☆ Favorite ⇄ Retweet ↰ Reply

@doctorow
Cory Doctorow

Been at the AA checkin desk for 2h now trying to sort out a Qantas points booking that Qantas totally screwed up, no help from Qantas

9 Sep via web ☆ Favorite ⇄ Retweet

@doctorow
Cory Doctorow

Anyone know a priority ph# for Qantas USA? We've been completely, totally screwed on a Qantas/AA reward ticket, 30+ mins on hold with Qantas

9 Sep via web ☆ Favorite ⇄ Retweet ↰ Reply

Provide customer feedback— griping and glowing

Twitter has become known as a place where forward-thinking companies provide customer service (we talk more about that in Chapter 6). But, like most things on Twitter, customer conversations go both ways. Which means you can use the medium to **let other people know about products you love and great service you've received—or about crappy products you've paid for and lousy experiences you've had.**

Often, particularly when you have a complaint, you can reach out directly to a company that provides customer service on Twitter, like UPS (@UPSHelp), Comcast (@ComcastCares), and many, many others, including small businesses. (Look on a company's website for their Twitter handle[s], or search Google for "*Company Name* Twitter").

Even if the company doesn't have an active customer service account you can find, your griping may attract its notice. When blogger Heather Armstrong (@dooce) bought a faulty washing machine from Maytag and was unable to get a satisfactory repair, she vented her frustration on Twitter—which resulted in a call from a company exec and a fix that day, plus a donation of a washer and dryer from Maytag competitor Bosch to a homeless shelter in Armstrong's town. Oh, and Maytag now has a customer service account on Twitter (@MaytagCare). (Armstrong's blog post on the incident: http://bit.ly/dooce-maytag.) You may not have the following she does, but you'd be surprised how often a tweet (or a heartfelt rant) can draw a company's response. Although Qantas missed the chance to help Cory Doctorow (@doctorow), shown here, they did send a nice note of apology afterward.

At least as important as complaining is complimenting. When you're really pleased with a company, share the love.

@mai
Mai Le

OH: a: "So, she was running the shower and crying for like an hour." b: "Oh my god, she ran the shower for an hour?"

3 Jul 10 via web   ☆ Favorite ⇄ Retweet ↩ Reply

@peretti
Jonah Peretti ✔

OH: We have a lotttttta money. That's our competitive advantage.

13 Sep via web   ☆ Favorite ⇄ Retweet ↩ Reply
from Paradise, NV

@jstogdill
Jim Stogdill

OH: After graduate school I went to Arthur Anderson. They had me do some shredding until Enron fired me.

24 Sep via Twitter for iPhone   ☆ Unfavorite ⇄ Retweet ↩ Reply

@SarahM
Sarah Milstein

OH in Queens: "Is it worse that I'm flirting with the bartender while my husband is away or that the bartender looks like my brother?"

30 Dec 08 via txt   ☆ Favorite ↩ Reply 🗑 Delete

Overhear things

Oddball conversations. One-sided cell phone calls. Funny comments. It's all **good fodder** for the already context-less world of Twitter.

You can just put quotes around the snippets. Or start your message with "Overheard" or "OH." (Incidentally, that works for your own thoughts.)

@lowflyingrocks
lowflyingrocks

1991 TF3, ~440m-990m in diameter, just passed the Earth at 14km/s, missing by ~twelve million, eight hundred thousand km.

2 hours ago via lowflyingrocks ☆ Favorite ⇄ Retweet ↩ Reply

@Genny_Spencer
Genevieve Spencer

Mr. Cape brought the ice cream freezer and some peaches. -July 3, 1939

26 Jul via TweetDeck ☆ Favorite ⇄ Retweet ↩ Reply

@wordnik
wordnik

Word of the Day: dogsbody: A person who does menial work, a servant. bit.ly/96OvuG #wotd

9 Sep via CoTweet ☆ Favorite ⇄ Retweet ↩ Reply

Publish on Twitter

By now, you've probably gotten the sense that Twitter is pretty much a blank canvas, waiting for you to fill it with cool stuff. Thing is, that stuff need not be limited to your own bon mots and retweets. In fact, **Twitter can serve very effectively as a publishing platform, letting you share regular posts on a theme.** Just a few of our favorites:

@Genny_Spencer, for a line a day from the 1937 diary of an Illinois farm girl, posted by her great-nephew.

@LowFlyingRocks, for announcements of every object that passes close to Earth.

@ThomasJefferson, for quotes from the author of the Declaration of Independence (for general quotes, try @IHeartQuotes).

@WordSpy and @wordnik, for new words and phrases.

twitter tip

Although we generally discourage automated posts for personal and business posting on Twitter, accounts like these are one of the places they can work well. To preschedule messages, try **SocialOomph** (http://socialoomph.com) or one of the third-party clients we discuss in Chapter 2.

@kanter
Beth Kanter ✔

Celebrating 25th Wedding Anniversary with a donation to @charitywater $25 gives clean water for 25 years bethkanter.org/relationships/

14 Sep via web   ☆ Favorite   ⇄ Retweet   ↩ Reply

@kabbenbock
Andy Smith

Become a Bone Marrow Donor: http://www.GetSwabbed.org/ and help complete item 2 on #alicebucketlist #getswabbed @100KCheeks

8 Jun via HootSuite   ☆ Favorite   ⇄ Retweet   ↩ Reply

@putthison
Put This On

We've broken $30,000 with four days left in our @Kickstarter campaign for season two. 727 backers. Let's go! kck.st/pYvxQI

11 Sep via Tweet Button   ☆ Favorite   ⇄ Retweet   ↩ Reply

Participate in fundraising campaigns

Twitter is the nexus for a fair amount of charitable fundraising. That is, people and organizations run campaigns in which you're asked to donate dollars (on another site) and perhaps donate a retweet, too. The success of these campaigns relies in large measure on the social fabric of Twitter—i.e., the strength of the connections people feel to each other. When enough Twitterers participate, **the numbers and awareness add up.**

Charity: water (http://www.charitywater.com), for example, has raised millions of dollars, much of it through Twitter-based campaigns and Twestival, a worldwide series of gatherings to benefit the organization. Meanwhile, projects that use **Kickstarter** (http://kickstarter.com), a site that helps people fund creative endeavors, very frequently use Twitter to get out the word.

If you see a campaign roll across your screen, consider participating and passing along the word. Of course, due diligence is always in order: at a minimum, check out the website of the organization sponsoring the event.

If you're looking to organize a campaign on Twitter, Beth Kanter (@bethkanter) has a blog (**"How Networked Nonprofits Are Using Social Media to Power Change,"** http://bethkanter.org) that can help you figure out what's worked, and what hasn't, in Twitter-based fundraising. Another good resource is **"The Dragonfly Effect: Quick, Effective, and Powerful Ways To Use Social Media to Drive Social Change,"** a very readable book by Jennifer Aaker (@aaker) and Andy Smith (@kabbenbock); http://www.dragonflyeffect.com.

@hannahmw23
Hannah Wallace

Happy #ff to fantastic Oregon-based writers & labor orgs: @foodshed, @nwlaborpress, @communal_table, @saludauction, @edibleportland

12 Aug via Seesmic for iPhone ☆ Favorite ⇄ Retweet

@MHarrisPerry
Melissa Harris-Perry

If you are not following my friend @JamilSmith then you are missing stories that matter and snark that tickles. #FollowFriday

27 May via TweetDeck ☆ Favorite ⇄ Retweet ↩ Reply

@SarahM
Sarah Milstein

It's Friday, so you really oughta follow @RepsLuvGov, pointed political insight peppered w/intriguing spousal commentary. #ff /cc @digiphile

9 Sep via web ☆ Favorite ↩ Reply 🗑 Delete

Make smart suggestions on FollowFriday

To **help each other find cool people to follow,** Twitterers have instituted FollowFriday. The idea couldn't be simpler: on Fridays, you post suggestions for accounts to follow, along with the hashtag #FollowFriday or #FF. (Reportedly, Micah Baldwin [@micah] started the trend back in the day.)

Trouble is people often post long lists of suggestions (well, as long as you can get in 140 characters) with no explanation. So on Fridays, don't be surprised to see messages scroll by that look like this:

"@cowbell400, @marketingbear, @pineconepeanuts, @superpoke2013, @thatsettlesit, @dubdubdubdc, @halliburton, @seatselectorfriend #FollowFriday"

Seriously, who's going to click through on those? Better to give a little context and list fewer folks. The examples here point you in the right direction.

twitter tip

As we mentioned earlier in this chapter, if you want your post to be seen by most people, don't start it with the @ symbol.

I wish crackbabies could appreciate how lucky they are. Getting their drugs for free the way they do.

@MrBrownEye2 14 minutes ago

 Raise your hand if you put walnuts in your brownies. Now use that hand and slap your face.

@badbanana 24 minutes ago

 "Denial, anger, bargaining, depression, acceptance." - five stages of grief/new Katy Perry song

@shelbyfero 32 minutes ago

Mark tweets as favorites
to draw attention to them

The juiciest tweets often have a life outside Twitter, most notably on sites that collect and highlight posts people have marked as favorites. These sites are handy for finding funny tweets and funny people on Twitter. They're also a way you can draw attention to tweets you particularly like, because when you mark one as favorite (described in Chapter 2), it will show up on these sites.

Try **Stellar** (http://stellar.io) for a good time perusing the things your friends are faving on Twitter, Flickr, Vimeo and YouTube. Like Twitter, Stellar lets you follow people—but in this case, all you see are things they've faved, and it winds up reading like a group blog of greatest hits. You can also track your own favorites or see your tweets, photos and videos that *other* people have faved. In addition, if you come across things on Stellar that you want to mark as favorite, you can do so right there, and they'll show up among your faves back on the original site (Twitter, Flickr, etcetera).

Favstar (http://favstar.fm) also integrates with your Twitter account (and no other services), but it's especially good at shining a light on what the rest of the world is faving on Twitter—much of it hilarious (and often raunchy). The Explore box on the left side of the page has a bunch of links to various popularity lists ("Tweets of the Day," "All Time," etcetera) that are worth a solid time-sink. The Leaderboard list is shown here.

"At a time of enormous problems, the politicians seem Lilliputian. That's the real reason to be afraid." http://www.economist.com/node/21530986?frsc=dg|a

RT @nelderini Why Richard Fisher dissented at the last FOMC meeting: http://stks.co/O2P via @EddyElfenbein

- My #strataconf conversation with @aneeshchopra: Government's Big Data Opportunity http://bit.ly/qDjFIJ My idea of "algorithmic regulation"

-Watched the first two episodes of Game of Thrones on the @virginamerica flight JFK-SFO. Almost does justice to the book.

The DIY Drones of @chr1sa at @ebmakerfaire on Oct 16t http://t.co/viwl5gjl

"our country faces a big choice: We can either have a hard decade or a bad century." http://nyti.ms/oLleGT

Wow, Elizabeth Warren just got my support in her Senate race. Big time common sense and straight talk! http://bit.ly/n4gkUW

The real digital divide: internet vs. talk radio listeners http://bit.ly/rsUuMq Top drive-time radio shows... via @pkedrosky

http://venturehacks.com/articles/option-pool-shuffle

100 Concise summaries of long-term thinking by Stewart Brand http://is.gd/TKLAQ8

-How to process a million songs in 20 minutes http://musicmachinery.com/2011/09/04/how-to-process-a-million-songs-in-20-minutes/ via @edd

Post on the right days and at the right times

A number of researchers have found that the most tweets are sent on Tuesdays, Wednesdays and Thursdays. While that may sound like a high-traffic time to avoid, it turns out that's when the most *retweets* are sent, too, suggesting **those are the days when people are most likely to pay attention to your messages.**

Similarly, for maximum exposure in the U.S., send messages during the afternoon Eastern Time. Of course, if you have a big international audience, save some tweets to send during *their* prime time or repeat yourself. (Many of the third-party clients covered in Chapter 2 let you preschedule tweets, as does **SocialOomph** [http://socialoomph.com].) Experiment to see what works best for you (Bit.ly, as covered in Chapter 6, helps you track click-throughs).

On the topic of scheduling tweets, we do recommend spacing your tweets out over the course of the day, rather than clumping them up. Because most people see your messages whenever they happen to look at Twitter (rather than going back and reading everything in their incoming timeline), you give yourself a greater change of reaching more people if you cover more hours. In addition, people are more likely to pay attention to your intermittent tweets rather than your big burst at, say, 8:00 a.m. (SocialFlow and Crowdbooster, both discussed in Chapter 6, try to figure out peak times for you.)

Incidentally, Tim spaces his post with a super low-tech method. He keeps a text file, shown here, where he forms tweets as he comes across interesting things. Then he posts them when he thinks they'll reach the right audience. On weekends, for example, he posts longer reads.

However you pre-form tweets, it's always smart to do so while you remember who pointed you to a link rather than leaving open a tab for days, and then forgetting how you found it.

@tarasophia
Tara Sophia Mohr

A few reasons to join #girleffect campaign: help girls in the developing world. meet fab bloggers. blog for good. taramohr.com/joinus/

7 Sep via web ☆ Favorite ↻ Retweet ↩ Reply

@tarasophia
Tara Sophia Mohr

For #girleffect bloggers: a great example of how you can spread the word about the campaign at your blog, starting now: musingbymoonlight.com/2011/08/24/an-...

☆ Favorite ↻ Retweet ↩ Reply

@tarasophia
Tara Sophia Mohr

From the everlovely @covetchicago. I can relate to her dilemma & am so glad she's a a part of @girleffect campaign! tinyurl.com/3gcf445

19 hours ago via Tweet Button ☆ Favorite ↻ Retweet ↩ Reply

@tarasophia
Tara Sophia Mohr

335 bloggers are signed up to blog about the @girleffect on October 4th. Want to join in the inspiration? taramohr.com/joinus/

2 hours ago via web ☆ Favorite ↻ Retweet ↩ Reply

Repost important tweets

One glorious aspects of Twitter is that, unlike email, it doesn't require a response—or even a glance. Indeed, many people treat it as a river of messages, dipping in when they happen to be next to the stream. **That behavior is important to understand** because it means that unless people see your message right away—sometimes as soon as five minutes within your posting—they're unlikely to see it at all. (Bit.ly, the URL-shortening service, has done an intriguing analysis of click-throughs: http://bit.ly/half-life-ctr.)

And *that* pattern is important to understand because it means that if you have something important to tweet about, it's a good idea to repeat yourself at least a couple of times, at different hours and probably over the course of several days. You might also create some anticipation by tweeting about important upcoming messages. And if you want the word to spread, you can ask for retweets (simply end the post with "Please retweet," as explained in Chapter 3).

Reposting can feel awkward at first, but you can do it artfully, especially if your message is clearly significant, non-commercial and not wildly self-promoting. And bear in mind that each message is just a sentence or two, so you're not imposing much on your followers. The example here gives you a sense of how to repost effectively and non-obnoxiously.

When you have an important message, consider emailing a few close compatriots and asking them to tweet it out, too. Provide a sample tweet that includes any relevant link, hashtag or info, and make sure it's no more than 140 characters. Of course, use this request sparingly with friends and colleagues. Think *very* hard before asking somebody who doesn't know you to tweet on your behalf—then, 99% of the time, decide not to ask.

CHAPTER 5 | Reveal Yourself

Twitter asks the question, "What's happening?" Although people now use Twitter to share the many kinds of ideas and information we describe in Chapter 4, they initially used it to answer that question pretty literally. So they reported that they were going for a bike ride, making bacon sundaes or watching the dog chew on a sofa cushion. Because they could send updates not only from their computers but from their phones, too, people also tweeted that they were sitting next to Bono on a flight to Zimbabwe, being handed a parking ticket on 5th Avenue or getting crummy service from United.

Although status updates like that may sound mundane, people on Twitter have found that **becoming aware of what your friends, family and colleagues are doing leads to a lightweight but meaningful intimacy.** Sociologists refer to this phenomenon as "co-presence," or the sense of being with others. Non-academics, when they have a name for it at all, call it "ambient intimacy" or, more commonly in work situations, "ambient awareness." You could think of it as a cross between ESP and what your mother might call "keeping in touch."

In this chapter, we look at things you can do to boost your personal connections on Twitter.

@gnat
Nat Torkington

Cancel the paternity test, Mr 12 just rhymed "brothel" with "ROFL".

13 Sep via Twitter for Mac ☆ Unfavorite ⇄ Retweet

@kenyatta
kenyatta cheese

When I go to former Eastern Bloc countries I think 'everyone is wearing the same thing' & then I come home & everyone is wearing blue jeans.

3 hours ago via Twitter for iPhone ☆ Favorite ⇄ Retweet ↩ Reply

@stephenfry
Stephen Fry ✓

Now THAT was a party. Goodness. Last time was up this late mobile phones were made of wood and brass.

11 Sep via Twitter for iPhone ☆ Favorite ⇄ Retweet ↩ Reply

Post personal updates

Whether you use Twitter primarily for professional reasons or personal reasons, **other people like little glimpses into your life**—probably more than you think. It helps them feel connected, it lends authenticity to your voice and it helps you build relationships. As a bonus, it means that when you see each other in person, instead of having a conversation that goes, "How've you been?" "Fine," you can have this conversation:

"Hey, saw that you were in Princeton last week. Did you have a chance to eat at Hoagie Haven?"

"Went twice—once for breakfast. Sounds like you've been busy with your new community garden. I used to have one when I lived in Brooklyn, and I loved it. How's yours going?"

Etcetera.

You don't have to reveal every little detail, but a few small updates can go a long way in fostering friendliness.

@lauraklein
Laura Klein

I swear, if it were not for conference calls from my home office, my toenails would never get painted.

8 May via web ☆ Favorite ⇄ Retweet ↩ Reply

@xenijardin
Xeni Jardin

FYI, I talked to some astronomers today and the correct pronunciation of ENCELADUS is "en-chi-LA-das." Saturn's "cheesy, mole-covered moon."

17 Sep via Twitter for iPhone ☆ Unfavorite ⇄ Retweet ↩ Reply

@backyardbeyond
Matthew Wills

Urban/nature interface: actually, that's not a black plastic bag in a tree, it's a crow.

22 Aug via web ☆ Unfavorite ⇄ Retweet ↩ Reply

Go beyond "What's happening?"

You don't have to limit your personal posts to answering the question, "What's happening?" You can **use your 140 characters to post thoughts, observations, advice, funny conversations, poetry, jokes, quotes,** etcetera.

You get the idea. (If you don't, we've included a few choice examples here.)

Use the right icon

There are a **couple of things to think about for your icon: fitting in and standing out.**

By "fitting in," we mean: if you want other people to recognize you as a friendly human on Twitter, use a photo or drawing that shows your face recognizably.

By "standing out," we mean: bear in mind that most people will see your tweets while they're glancing at a slew of messages. You can see here that the faces on the left grab you more readily than most of the less-clear icons on the right. Play around with your icon until you hit on a variation that will help people find you—and relate to you—in Twitter's small format.

You can find the icon upload under Profile › "Edit your profile".

Amanda Jones
@AmandaJones91

Hilary Mason
@hmason NYC

chief scientist @bitly. Machine learning; I ♥ data and cheeseburgers.
http://www.hilarymason.com

Fill out your full bio (it takes two seconds)

When you sign up for Twitter, the system asks you just for your name and username. So it's easy to blow off the rest of your profile settings, which include your location, a URL for you and a brief bio. But **other people like those details,** so jump in and add them.

Bonus: the more information you share, the less you look like a spammer. To wit: which of the accounts shown here are you more likely to follow?

In Chapter 1, we give tips on filling out your profile, which you can find under Profile → "Edit your profile".

Eric Ries

@ericries SF

Trying to change how startups are built.
http://startuplessonslearned.com/

Amy Jo Kim

@amyjokim Burlingame, CA

Game Designer, Bass Player, Mom
http://shufflebrain.com

Prof. Sree
Sreenivasan
Dean of Student
Affairs, Columbia
Journalism
School
www.Sree.net

SOCMEDIA GUIDE
bit.ly/sreesoc

FACEBOOK PAGE,
FILLED
WITH TIPS:
Facebook.com/
sreetips

TECH WORKSHOPS:
bit.ly/workshops

WEBCASTS:
* BlogTalkRadio.com/
columbiajournalism
* BlogTalkRadio.com/
saja
* BlogTalkRadio.com/
sreetips

E-mail me (and
ask to be on
my monthly
tips list):
sree@sree.net

Sree

@sree N

@Columbia
http://ww
evangelist/
tech, media
http://sree.n

   ✓ Following

Tweet to @sree

Tweets   Favorites   Following ▾

 sree Sree Sreenivasan
NEW TO ME: Recomm
interesting users on Goo
1 hour ago

 sree Sree Sreenivasan
#MUSTREAD: What Fac
Twitter, by @mathewi in
23 Sep

 sree Sree Sreenivasan
[Twitpic] Smart use of p.

Prof. Sree
Sreeni
Dean o
Affairs
Journa
School
www.S

SOCMED
bit.ly/s

FACEBO
FILLED
WITH TI
Faceboo
sreetips

TECH W
bit.ly/w

WEBCAS
* BlogT
columbi
* BlogT
saja
* BlogT
sreetips

E-mail
ask to
my mo
tips lis
sree@

Sree

@sree N

@Columbia
http://ww
evangelist/
tech, media
http://sree.n

✓ Following

Tweet to @sree

Tweets   Favorites   Following ▾

 sree Sree Sreenivasan
NEW TO ME: Recomm
interesting users on Goo
1 hour ago

sree Sree Sreenivasan
#MUSTREAD: What Fac
Twitter, by @mathewi in
23 Sep

sree Sree Sreenivasan
[Twitpic] Smart use of p.

Spiff up your background

Twitter lets you customize the *background* of your account page. Recently, though, they changed the layout of the page so that on most screens, you can see just a snippet of the background—making that customization a lot less fun and important. Still, because on larger screens in particular people will see your background, consider tweaking it to **bring some additional personality to your page.**

If you do nothing, your page looks like the upper example here (Eric Ries's page)—which isn't bad. If you want to take it another step, you can change just the colors (background, sidebar, links and outlines), or you can choose one of several nifty themes Twitter has created for your backgrounding pleasure. You can also upload your own background photo, as you can see on Amy Jo Kim's page here. Take care of all the visual tweaks under Settings → Design.

While it's a great idea to provide more info, as Sree Sreenivasan has done here, you can see that on smaller screens (the right-hand example), the background gets cut off. So be it; it's still good practice to give people more insight into who you are and how they can reach you. **TwitBacks** (http://twitbacks.com) is one choice for creating an informative background. (Note that the text in a background image can't have live links, so it's still a good idea to provide at least some other contact info in your bio, covered in Chapter 1).

@bonniedone
Bonnie Duncan

RT @danmil 3 plane rides, 2 multihour drives, visit to grand and great grandmother's houses & 1 wedding later, all 5 of us are home. Phew #fb

11 Sep via Twitterrific ☆ Favorite ⇄ Retweet ↩ Reply

facebook   Search   🔍

Bonnie Duncan
RT @danmil 3 plane rides, 2 multihour drives, visit to grand and great grandmother's houses & 1 wedding later, all 5 of us are home. Phew

⚑ Like · Comment · September 11 at 10:12pm via Selective Tweets · ✳

👍 Sada Sat Kaur and 3 others like this.

Cross-post to Facebook, LinkedIn, and more

As you have probably noticed, Twitter updates and Facebook status updates are a lot alike. Given the similarity, it may make sense to cross-post and **have messages you send out on Twitter also show up on Facebook.** There are two common reasons you might cross-post:

1. You tend to be inactive on Facebook, so feeding in tweets livens up your Facebook presence.

2. You use Facebook to connect with a lot of casual acquaintances, and feeding in tweets lets you collect a lot of comments.

Many third-party Twitter clients let you cross-post to other accounts (see Chapter 2 for a few recommendations). You can also use a Facebook app to help you out. **Selective Twitter Status** (http://apps.facebook.com/selectivetwitter/) lets you choose which tweets also post to Facebook; once you've installed it, you just add #fb to any tweet that you want to cross-post, as shown here. **The Twitter Facebook app** (http://apps.facebook.com/twitter/) cross-posts all of your tweets.

The same principles of cross-posting apply to other networks that allow status updates, like LinkedIn. To post simultaneously across a bunch of social networking sites, try **Ping.fm** (http://ping.fm). For LinkedIn only, edit your profile on LinkedIn; click "Add Twitter account."

Note that most cross-posting services don't include tweets that start with the @ symbol, nor do they include things posted via Twitter's Retweet button (explained in Chapter 3).

@ericries
Eric Ries

Hello NYC! Anyone interested in an impromptu book signing tomorrow (Sat)?

23 Sep via Twitter for iPhone   ☆ Favorite   ↻ Retweet   ↩ Reply

from Queens
New York, US
View Tweets about this place

@sgdean
Steven Dean

Sardines, crepes, nutella. Not in that order. (@ Bastille Day On 60th Street w/ 138 others) http://4sq.com/pw8hU2

10 Jul via foursquare   ☆ Favorite   ↻ Retweet   ↩ Reply

Divulge your location

Because a lot of tweeting happens when you're out and about, **it's natural to bake your location into at least some posts.** Twitter has a feature to let you add your general location—determined by your browser or mobile device—into individual tweets as you choose. The top tweet here shows you an example of what that looks like, with a little map and the label "from Queens, New York, US," which suggest Eric Ries just landed at a New York City airport. You can also use third-party services like **Foursquare** (http://foursquare.com) or **Gowalla** (http://gowalla.com) to "check in" at any location, including events and specific addresses, and then share that via Twitter. In the bottom tweet, the location info in parentheses and the 4sq.com URL are your big hints that this message was posted via Foursquare.

While adding location information can provide context to a tweet and can help people find you, it can, well, help people find you. Obviously, that can impinge on your privacy and safety. Be thoughtful about the locations you divulge.

With that in mind, Twitter's geolocation feature is turned off by default. To turn it on, simply attempt to add your location to a tweet by clicking in the "What's happening?" box, and then clicking the little crosshair icon that appears below the box; when you do so, Twitter opens a box offering more info on the location option and providing a button to enable it.

If you use one of the third-party apps, like Foursquare, to share your location on Twitter, do everyone a favor and add a useful or funny comment. The default text—"I'm at W Chicago (644 N Lake Shore Dr, at Ontario St., Chicago) w/ 16 others" offers your followers little or nothing of value.

O'REILLY radar
Insight, analysis, and research about emerging technologies

Four short links: 27 September 2011
Source Code, SPDY Trials, Data from Facebook, and Voting Tools

by Nat Torkington | @gnat | 27 September 2011

The New York Times

OP-ED COLUMNIST

A Few Words With Iran's President

By NICHOLAS D. KRISTOF
Published: September 21, 2011

Before sparks began flying between me and President Mahmoud

~~Ahmadinejad of Iran, he began my interview with an unusual olive~~

Then the interview was over, and Mr. Ahmadinejad zoomed back from bombast to conciliation. He beamed and told me: "We truly like and love the people of the United States."

For a transcript of my interview with President Ahmadinejad, visit my blog, On the Ground. Please also join me on Facebook and Google+, watch my YouTube videos and follow me on Twitter.

Post your Twitter handle widely

If you want people to find and follow you on Twitter, you can give them a big boost by posting your Twitter handle (i.e., your @username) a number of key places:

1. In the signature file of your email messages. Most email programs won't turn your @username into a link, so you may want to include the URL, like so: http://twitter.com/YourUsername. DO NOT include a request for somebody to follow you in the body of an email; it's obnoxious, at best.

2. On your blog or other places you post. If you include your Twitter handle everywhere you write or post stuff, you make it *much* easier for people to share your links and give you credit. In the ideal setup, your @username appears with every post (along with info like your real name). Check out the way we do it on the O'Reilly Radar group blog (http://radar.oreilly.com), shown here. The *New York Times* puts the info at the bottom of the page for selected columnists, though this method requires readers click around to get the @username. Indeed, posting a link that says, "Follow me on Twitter" rather than your @username is akin to giving out conference nametags that say, "Ask me my name."

You can also add your most recent tweets to your site with widgets from Twitter (http://twitter.com/widgets). Though this isn't a bad idea generally, we don't recommend it as a way of publicizing your @username, for the reason mentioned above. If you write for a site that doesn't post @usernames, ask that it be included in your bio.

3. On conference badges. If the event organizers don't automatically include it, write in your @username by hand.

CHAPTER 6 | Twitter for Business: Special Considerations and Ideas

If you're tweeting on behalf of your company, non-profit organization or in a primarily professional capacity, you've got a few additional challenges to make your Twitter account successful. In fact, everything we've said already applies to you. Here we discuss **additional considerations and ideas to make your company's or organization's tweeting really sing.**

Incidentally, if you're interested in *internal* status updates for your organization—which a lot of companies find to be an inbox-freeing revelation—check out **Yammer** (http://yammer.com).

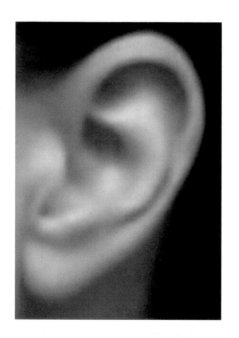

Listen first

The **biggest mistake we see companies make when they first hit Twitter** is to think about it as a channel to push out information. In fact, it turns out to be a great medium for holding *conversations* rather than for making announcements.

People already on Twitter will expect your corporate account(s) to engage with them, so before you start tweeting away, spend a few weeks or so understanding the ways people talk about you. Get a sense for the rhythms of conversation on Twitter, and think about how you'll hold conversations.

No matter your sector, chances are that people are already tweeting about your products, your brand, your company or at least your industry. In Chapter 2, we cover a range of listening tools and techniques; later in this chapter, we address a few more.

twitter tip

Some companies and consultants build customer relationships by keeping an eye on Twitter search for questions they can answer, and then carefully approaching the person who's asked the question. If you use this method, be sensitive to the fact that people might not want to hear from you.

What will be different in three months, six months or a year **because we've engaged on Twitter?**

Have clear goals

Because it's so lightweight, Twitter may tempt you to just dive in and give it a try. Which is a reasonable approach if you're an individual.

But **for companies, an unfocused stab at tweeting can lead to accounts that don't represent the business well or that conflict with other communication channels.** Twitter is littered with corporate accounts that somebody started with good intentions but then abandoned after a short period, leaving a permanent, public record of corporate neglect. In addition, tweeting can suck up staff time; why assign resources to Twitter if you don't know what you're hoping to get out of it?

Twitter gives you an unparalleled opportunity to build relationships with customers and other constituents, and we suggest you think of it in those terms, rather than as part of a campaign. That said, you can do yourself a big favor by spending some time thinking through what you'd most like to get out of your account or accounts and whether you'll measure that (we talk more about measurement later in this chapter).

Your goals might include things like better serving your existing customers, increasing your customer base, offering customer service, connecting with potential partners and so forth.

@WholeFoods
Whole Foods Market ●

Have a pic of your baby's first good food experience? Check out The First Yum™ Baby Photo Contest on our Facebook page! http://cot.ag/hBOnDQ

7 Mar via CoTweet ☆ Favorite ⇄ Retweet ↩ Reply

@WholeFoods
Whole Foods Market ●

@JeremiahLowery1 Can you please email your question to Michael.bepko@wholefoods.com?

21 hours ago via CoTweet ☆ Favorite ⇄ Retweet ↩ Reply

Integrate with your other channels

Twitter is cool, but it's not magic. It's part of your communications toolkit, and it probably fits with at least a few of your departments or functions: customer service, PR, marketing, product development, human resources, etcetera—all of whom are already using a bunch of tools to connect with people.

For instance, you may think of your account as an information booth where you share tips, links, promos and so forth, but people will likely come to you with questions and complaints. You still need a way to respond to those customers appropriately, perhaps from within your customer service department. We've too often seen corporate accounts that post messages like, "@customer: That's a shame. Email us for help." And then there's no email address given. For a customer who's already having a problem, that sort of reply simply amps up her frustration. Much better to provide specific contact info, or even take the conversation to DM, get the customer's contact info, and then have customer service follow up.

To have accounts that truly engage on behalf of your company, make sure people throughout your organization are aware of any corporate tweeting and that you have some basic systems set up to route and resolve inquiries and complaints. Of course, if you spend time listening, as we recommend earlier in this chapter, you'll be able to plan ahead for the kinds of queries you might need to field.

In addition to integrating with your departments, coordinate your Twitter, Facebook and other social media accounts to provide consistent information.

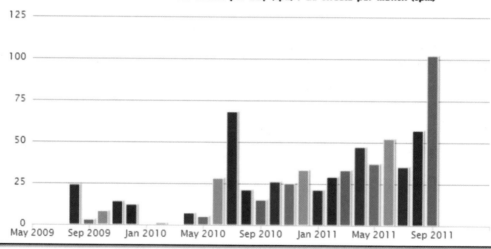

TweetStats for BerginoBaseball (Tweet This!)
Last updated 29 Sep 2011 at 14:17

Your Tweet Timeline – 1.8 tweets per day (tpd) / 29 tweets per month (tpm)

Start slow, then build

A big concern execs—and pretty much everyone—has about Twitter is that it will be **a black hole of time for employees.** And it can be.

To avoid that problem altogether, start slow, posting perhaps once a day or just a few times a week and answering questions several times a day. Then, if the account proves useful, start devoting more time and resources to it. If it doesn't pan out, you haven't put a hard-to-justify amount of time into it.

Here we use **TweetStats** (http://tweetstats.com) to look at the Twitter activity for @BerginoBaseball, the account for a company that sells handmade baseballs and has popular store and gallery in Manhattan. They started slowly, found Twitter to be a useful tool, and then amped up their posting.

@Benioff
Marc Benioff

I'm very excited about Thursday night with @jayleno @morissette @MCHammer and @iamwill at the SF Symphony Hall theconcertforucsfbch.com C U There

30 Aug via Twitter for Mac   ☆ Favorite   ⇄ Retweet   ↶ Rep

@Benioff
Marc Benioff

Salesforce is hiring Accnt Execs and Enginrs worldwide. Send your cv to wmartin@salesforce.com. Our vision: bit.ly/qwfpEP

@ariannahuff
Arianna Huffington ✔

Noah Michelson for @HuffingtonPost Gay Voices: "There's a lot to celebrate... and there's a lot of work left to do."
huffingtonpost.com/noah-michelson...

22 hours ago via web   ☆ Favorite   ⇄ Retweet   ↶ Reply

Figure out who does the tweeting

Twitter is a social medium. So **if you have to choose between a person who has perfect information to share but doesn't really get or like tweeting, and a person who totally embraces the medium,** choose the latter. Then find a way to support that person with extra information and access to the people who tend to be your knowledge hubs. Of course, in many cases, particularly in larger companies, you'll have multiple employees who tweet; we talk more about that later in this chapter.

Incidentally, we can't recommend outsourcing your tweeting to a PR firm, ad agency or marketing consultancy. While that might appear to be an appealing time-saver, it's highly unlikely to yield the kinds of relationships that customers expect, and it could easily backfire if people get the feeling that they're being talked to by an inauthentic representative or that they're being sold to.

In fact, many of the most successful users of Twitter are also the busiest. Some executives, like Acumen Fund CEO Jacqueline Novogratz (@jnovogratz) and Huffington Post co-founder and president Arianna Huffington (@ariannahuff), mostly share information from their companies or related to areas in which they do business; others, like Cisco CTO Padmasree Warrior (@padmasree) and Best Buy CEO Brian J. Dunn (@BBYCEO), share a lot of snapshots from their lives. But it doesn't have to be an either/or deal: Martha Stewart (@marthastewart) and Salesforce.com CEO Marc Benioff (@benioff) do both well.

Bill Gerth ✔

@comcastcares Philadelphia, PA
My name is Bill Gerth also known as @comcastbill. *We are here to Make it Right for our customers. William_Gerth@comcast.com*
http://www.comcast.com

Reveal the person behind the curtain

The **biggest opportunity Twitter gives you is the chance to show the personality and humanness behind your organization.** When you do so, you create the Petri dish in which you can grow conversations with people and establish relationships on a relatively intimate level.

After all, people like connecting with people more than with a nameless, faceless entity. So once you've decided who's going to do the tweeting for your company, be sure to name him or her on your Twitter account page. In your profile settings (under Profile → "Edit your profile"), use the Name field to identify the company, and then use the 160-character Bio to identify the person or people behind the account.

The Comcast customer support account shown here (@comcastcares) goes a step farther. It features not only full info about the person behind the account, including his own Twitter handle and email address, but also a *picture* of him rather than a corporate logo. Because it makes it less clear who owns the account, we don't recommend using a staff name in the Name field, as he's done here (instead, use a company name and put the staff name in the bio). But the rest of the info is so helpful and terrific, we couldn't resist including this example.

PR Newswire

@PRNewswire Global

Vicky, Director, Audience Development & team: @victoriaharres @cpcube ^cc @savsimon ^bss @thomashynes ^th. We talk #media #socialmedia #journalism #PR #Mktg!

http://www.prnewswire.com

Tweet to @PRNewswire

Tweets   Favorites   Following ▾   Followers ▾   Lists ▾

 PRNewswire PR Newswire
The Newsonomics of Disruption: bit.ly/oYlB7K via @NiemanLab ^th
2 minutes ago

 PRNewswire PR Newswire

Manage multiple staffers on one account

If you've got more than one person tweeting from an account, **you need a way to identify the crew.** It's a good idea to have a two-pronged approach:

1. Include names in the 160-character bio (you can edit it under Profile → "Edit your profile"). That field is the place where search engines look for information, and it's also the place Twitter draws from to represent your account in third-party clients (described in Chapter 2). Of course, 160 characters isn't much room, and you may wind up just listing first names and perhaps the team department.

2. Sign messages with the initials of whomever is posting. Just prefix the initials with a piece of punctuation, like the carat symbol, to signal that it's a signature.

Check out the PR Newswire account (@PRNewswire), which lists the four people who tweet from the account, their personal Twitter handles, and their initials, which they use to sign tweets. When people connect with this account, they really know who they're getting.

By the way, at the end of this chapter, we talk about Co-Tweet, which is a useful tool for keeping a bunch of people coordinated on one account.

Arts

 NYTimes Arts
 Follow
The latest news in arts and entertainment.

 NYTimes Music
 Follow
The latest in music reviews and news.

 NYTimes TV
Follow
News and reviews from the world of television.

 ArtsBeat
 Follow @artsbeat
Blogging from arts reporters and critics.

 NYTimes Theater
Follow
News, reviews and showtimes for Broadway, Off Broadway and London.

 Dave Itzkoff
Follow @ditzkoff
Culture Reporter, ArtsBeat

 Jonathan Landman
Follow
Culture Editor

 Jon Pareles
Follow
Music Critic

 Ben Sisario
Follow @sisario
Media Reporter

 Julie Bloom
Follow @Julesbm
Assistant Editor, Arts

 A.O. Scott
Follow @aoscott
Film Critic

 Erik Piepenburg
Follow
Senior Producer, Arts

 Mekado Murphy
 Follow
Producer, Arts

Autos

 Wheels
 Follow
Blogging about all things automotive.

 James G. Cobb
 Follow
Automobiles Editor

Books

 NYTimes Books

 Paper Cuts

Pamela Paul

Coordinate multiple accounts

It's one thing to have multiple people tweeting from the same organizational account, but what if you've got a bunch of corporate accounts? **Identify your array of accounts on an easy-to-find web page** to help people discover them and understand which ones will be of interest.

As you can see here, the *New York Times*—which has dozens of Twitter accounts, plus staffers with their own accounts—has grouped them all on one page, and then shown the icon and a description for each. You can see the whole list at http://nytimes.com/twitter.

Another option is to create a Twitter list (described in Chapter 2), add all of your staffers to it, and list that in your bio. JetBlue (@JetBlue) does that. If you want to see the list, check out http://twitter.com/jetblue/team.

twitter tip

To help people find and understand your various accounts, have them follow, talk to and cc each other. They can retweet one another, refer to each other, and exchange messages. No need to overdo it, but don't avoid interaction either.

Fab

@Fab

Fab.com features daily design inspirations and sales at up to 70% off retail.
http://fab.com

Tweets   Favorites   Following ▾   Followers ▾   Lists ▾

Fab Fab
Fab.com Flash Sale: Phase Design Limited quantity.
fab.com/sale/1226/izue... via @Fab
9 minutes ago

Fab Fab
@jivinivan We have to verify that your invitees finished creating their account - it can take up to 24 hours to do that.
2 hours ago

Fab Fab
@abbisiler They are really cute!
3 hours ago

Fab Fab
@ashleyv it's working for us. What happens when you click Google+?
3 hours ago

Be conversational

As we discuss earlier in this chapter, Twitter is a terrific medium for conversation, and it's what people on the system expect. In fact, if you refrained from one-way PR blasts and instead participated in lots of exchanges, you'd be **using Twitter in a way that you can't do with any other communication channels.**

What does conversation look like? A lot of @messages, as described in Chapters 1 and 3. This Fab account is a good example: see how three of the four most recent messages are @replies? Increasingly, corporate and organizational accounts look like this.

(Remember: @replies are usually seen only by people following both parties to the conversation. So if you want your reply to be seen by all your followers, don't put the @ at the very beginning of the tweet. For more on this important issue, see Chapter 4.)

@MuseumModernArt
Museum of Modern Art

Thanks! RT @brainpicker: Really, really loving the redesign of @MuseumModernArt's MoMA/PS1 Inside/Out blog http://j.mp/mdjDlA

7 Jun via TweetDeck ☆ Favorite ⏄ Retweet ↰ Reply
from New York City, NY

@VirginAmerica
Virgin America ✓

Can your airline do this? RT @ryanstarfan I am currently watching tv, on WiFi, chatting, tweeting & flying on @VirginAmerica all at once! :)

21 hours ago via Sprinklr ☆ Favorite ⏄ Retweet ↰ Reply

@DonorsChoose
DonorsChoose ✓

This is amazing! Y'all rock! RT @Kevin_Church: YOU DID IT. You and other people helped a school rebuild its library! t11.me/O6Z-H4

18 Aug via Tap11 ☆ Favorite ⏄ Retweet ↰ Reply

@randomdeanna
Deanna Zandt

aw, @WSKG rt'ed me. glowy feeling when the station that intro'ed me to jazz & Hitchhiker's Guide to the Galaxy thinks i'm nifty. ;-)

8 Sep via Twitter for Mac ☆ Unfavorite ⏄ Retweet ↰ Reply

Retweet your customers

As we discuss in Chapters 1 and 3, retweeting is an essential part of the way people hold conversations on Twitter. **To really be part of the community,** then, do as the Romans do and retweet people.

Doing so shows people respect and amplifies their voices—both great actions for building relationships. Often, a quick thanks (as in the Museum of Modern Art [@MuseumModernArt] example here) or acknowledging a happy customer (as in the Virgin America [@VirginAmerica] example) is all it takes to give somebody a little thrill. DonorsChoose.org (@DonorsChoose) is a non-profit that helps teachers raise funds for classroom projects; in this retweet, the organization shares a donor's excitement over a successful campaign.

For good measure, we've included an example from Deanna Zandt (@randomdeanna), who really appreciated being retweeted by a radio station she likes.

jen14221 Jennifer Wutz-Lopes
An earlier flight but $40? Really @JetBlue? Come on. You can sell my 6pm seat for $300. 4sq.com/mSAeGg
2 hours ago

in reply to @jen14221 ↑

@JetBlue
JetBlue Airways ✓

@jen14221 You can fly standby one flight prior to your scheduled flight for no charge. bit.ly/pWTVd2 #buffy

2 hours ago via CoTweet   ☆ Favorite   ⟲ Retweet   ↩ Reply

@gnat
Nat Torkington

Ah, looks like @wooshnewzealand doesn't do customer support through twitter. Another reason not to choose them.

28 Sep via Twitter for Mac   ☆ Unfavorite   ⟲ Retweet   ↩ Reply

Offer solid customer support

As we discuss earlier in this chapter, whether you set up your account with customer service in mind, you'll likely get such inquiries. The cool thing about Twitter is that **you can reply in public,** demonstrating your company's responsiveness. Even better, if one person asks a question, it's likely a bunch of people have the same issue, so answering publicly can help a lot of folks at once. (Of course, some inquiries are specialized; take those to DM.)

In addition to direct questions you get, keep an eye on Twitter search (see Chapter 2) and respond to complaints or concerns about your company, as shown here. If you approach people like this, do so gently; some will be pleased to hear from you, others may find it a bit creepy.

If your company has a very high volume of customer service messages, consider opening an account or several just for customer service. @ComcastCares is one just example of many.

twitter tip

Earlier in this chapter, we talk about the importance of making sure that the person or people running your Twitter account are integrated with your customer service arm. Otherwise, you can easily create more steps for customers who are trying to resolve problems.

 **@20x200**
20x200

TONIGHT! The NY Art Book Fair kicks off with a preview from 6-9pm. Catch it this weekend, thru 10/2 @MoMAPS1: bit.ly/nVClI1

4 hours ago via CoTweet   ☆ Favorite ⇄ Retweet

 **@justfood**
Just Food

Want to start an Urban Farm? @UnitedWayNYC & HPNAP have Seed Grants for you! Check out the application at www.feednyc.org Deadline: Oct. 4!

26 Sep via TweetDeck   ☆ Favorite ⇄ Retweet ↩ Reply

 **@thehipmunk**
hipmunk

Heading to Europe and want to save some moolah ?? @michellehiggins @nytimes has the scoop: travel.nytimes.com/2011/10/02/tra...

28 Sep via web   ☆ Favorite ⇄ Retweet ↩ Reply

Post mostly NOT about your company

Kathy Sierra has said, "With few exceptions, the worst mistake a 'business blog' can make is to blog about the business." The same principle holds true in Twitter.

If you're a brand that a lot of people already adore, you can probably get away with posting mostly about your own company—people love you, and they want more. But if you're an unknown entity to most people, or if you have a mixed reputation, or if you just want to take your Twitter relationships to another level, **think about Twitter as a way to exchange mutually interesting information.**

So rather than post a lot of information about your company, aim instead to post mostly third-party links, resources and tips that would be of interest to people who follow you. The examples shown here do exactly that. 20x200 (@20x200) is a company, based in New York, with an innovative model for selling art online. Alerting followers to a local art show is a natural fit. Likewise, Just Food (@justfood), a non-profit that has a program to help urban gardeners grow food, posts information about a grant that its community might well want to investigate. And Hipmunk (@thehipmunk) is a travel search site, so you'd expect its followers to be interested in the story they link to here.

Taking this approach helps build your credibility with customers, potential customers and other constituents. It also makes you a more likely go-to source for journalists.

@LearnVest
LearnVest

LV Tip of the Day: You could earn back the cost of a new refrigerator in a few years, just through electricity saved: http://ow.ly/6IRhp

3 hours ago via HootSuite ☆ Favorite ⏱ Retweet ↩ Reply

@Etsy
Etsy ✓

"When my son's 1st grade teacher told him to act normal, he asked: "You want me to be a setting on the dryer?" etsy.me/pDDqky

3 hours ago via CoTweet ☆ Favorite ⏱ Retweet ↩ Reply

@LPFI
Level Playing Field

Looking for an excuse to go to the @exploratorium WITHOUT your kids? Look no further. Join us on Oct 20 at 7pm lpfi.org/fairness-matte...

21 Sep via web ☆ Favorite ⏱ Retweet ↩ Reply

Link creatively to your own sites

Even if you use Twitter primarily to post information that's not directly about your company, you can—and should—use it to sometimes link back to your own site or blog. Many companies find that Twitter can become a top referrer to their sites, so avail yourself of that benefit—just do it in a smart way.

The key is to frame the link in a way that's interesting to your Twitter followers. So instead of saying, "New Blog Post: Mundane Headline, http://yourblog.com," try something like the examples here, each of which links back to the organizations' own sites or blogs.

twitter tip

If you're looking to get the most out of Twitter, don't fall into the trap of posting an RSS feed of headlines from your site or blog. Although there are services that will automate such a connection for you, they simply help you create an impersonal account that duplicates the main feature of an RSS reader. Why bother?

@DellOutlet
Dell Outlet ✔

Save 20% off all Dell Outlet Printers!
Enter VSW1B86FB0NVWM at checkout:
del.ly/6011RTWL (limit 2/cust ,exp 9/24,
not stackable)

22 Sep via Sprinklr ☆ Favorite ⨯ Retweet ↩ Reply

@DWR_Tweets
Design Within Reach

Interested in winning a $500 DWR Gift
Card? Enter the Dining Room Design
Contest by end of day Tuesday.
bit.ly/qXtlUc

@Dropbox
Dropbox

The Inaugural Dropquest scavenger hunt
is now live! Win free space and fantastic
prizes for being smart! http://bit.ly
/haPJB5

15 Jan via web ☆ Favorite ⨯ Retweet ↩ Reply

@Seamless
Seamless

A quick #STrivia rules refresher: 1
winner/question; 1 answer per
person/question; 1 win/day per person.
$10 on Seamless for each win!

9 hours ago via TweetDeck ☆ Favorite ⨯ Retweet ↩ Reply

Make money with Twitter

Because Twitter can drive a lot of traffic to your sites, think hard about how you can **use it to help people find good deals you offer.** Among the successful tactics companies use:

1. Promotions. Offer Twitter-specific discount codes. Some companies report that lower-priced items are much more likely to get uptake. Do some testing to see what works for you.

2. Contests. The Twitterverse has seen a lot of contests. But people do tend to like them, and fun, creative games with good rewards can generate some nice buzz. (If you run a contest, be sure to describe it on your website and include legal details.)

3. Sale announcements. Let people know when you run a great sale. Or if you run an outlet, post choice new items as they hit your inventory.

By the way, contests and solid deals tend to get retweeted, so they can be a good way of drawing not just business, but legitimate new followers, too. Also, if you offer deals, try posting them a number of times to get on the radar of a lot of people.

Your Tweets **10,163**

1 hour ago · ⟲ **w2e** We're officially SOLD OUT of Web ...

Following **374**   Followers **11,954**

age →

all

ment.

Who to follow · refresh · view all

 bing Bing ✔ · Follow   ✕
↗ Promoted · Followed by @BillGates and others

 michaelmurray MICHAEL MURRAY · Follow   ✕
Social Media Scientist for @RyanSeacrest, @1027K...

 GavinNewsom Gavin Newsom ✔ · Follow   ✕
Followed by @bjfogg and others.

Trends: United States · change

#McDMonopoly ↗ Promoted

#ThatHighMoment

Hello October

Cooper Stone

Advertise on Twitter...maybe

With hundreds of millions of users monthly, many of them talking about things they're interested in, places they're going and people they're connected to, **the Twitter site can be an attractive place to advertise.** The hitch is that of the three ways Twitter has introduced so far to let you run ads, only one is currently open to anyone; the other two are in a closed beta (meaning a they're in a test phase with a small number of users). You can find all three (and sign up for the betas), plus get information on an analytics package for advertisers, at http://business.twitter.com. Here's the rundown:

1. Promoted Accounts. This is the program that's open right now. It lets you buy a spot that appears in the Who To Follow section of the site and in search results. The top example here shows what it looks like, with a promoted account for Bing. The little yellow arrow and the word "Promoted" are your hints that this isn't organic. This might be a good choice if you're planning a big push from your account, and you want to boost followers beforehand.

2. Promoted Tweets. These show up in search results (as shown in Chapter 2) and in users' timelines (though we have yet to see that in the wild). This could be a good way to go if you're trying to draw attention to something strongly associated with a particular keyword.

3. Promoted Trends. Shown in the lower example here, these appear at the top of the Trends list. Because the trending topics are associated with buzz and fast-moving issues, this could be a good option for product launches and events.

@thebostonshaker
thebostonshaker

Holy crazy morning, Batman! Looks like our website is down! So sorry for the inconvenience. We're getting @tricomRI on it ASAP!

14 Sep via HootSuite

@thebostonshaker
thebostonshaker

Website's back up! Everything *seems* to be normal, but let us know if you see any issues. Thanks for the offers of help, y'all!

14 Sep via HootSuite   ☆ Unfavorite ↻ Retweet ↩ Reply

Report problems...and resolutions

Twitter is a great place to acknowledge that your company is having some kind of problem. Your site is down. Your conference hotel ballroom is flooded. One of your stores has run out of Cabbage Patch Kids. **Letting people know that you're aware of the issue— and that it may be causing them some pain—is just good, human service.**

Of course, Twitter also gives you the chance to let people know you've rectified the situation.

@omnivorebooks
Omnivore Books

Sometimes, love just hits like a bolt from the blue. twitpic.com/6oxjp8

 TwitPic

22 Sep via Twitpic

@food52
food52

OH @food52: "Ugh, chinchillas are horrible." "We've had this conversation before."

23 Aug via web ☆ Favorite ⇄ Retweet ↩ Reply
from New York, NY

Post personal updates

As we said earlier in this chapter, **Twitter gives you a phenomenal chance to reveal the human side of your organization,** helping people connect with a person or people who work for you. That starts with identifying your staffers on Twitter. The next step is posting the occasional personal update.

The personal updates don't have to be constant, and it's fine if they're work-related. But do add them in sometimes, as your followers like getting them a lot more than you probably expect.

For instance, Omnivore Books (@omnivorebooks) is a culinary bookstore—but followers loved this picture of a customer's puppy. Food52 (@food52), a cooking site, has nothing to do with chinchillas, but this snippet of an overheard conversation gives followers a funny glimpse behind the scenes.

You might be surprised, but little posts like that can go a long way toward building relationships.

What If Male Superheroes Posed Like Wonder Woman On The David Finch Justice League Cover? Bleeding Cool Comic Book, Movies and TV News and Rumors

145 Clicks
This bitly link *bit.ly/qLZFC1* was added by sgmils

837 Clicks
All clicks on the aggregate bitly link *bit.ly/r16Cmr* | Info Page+

Long Link: http://www.bleedingcool.com/2011/08/05/what-if-male-superheroes-posed-like-wonder-woman-on-the-david...
Conversations: Tweets **2**, Shares **0**, Likes **4**, Comments **0**,   View All

145 Click(s) on this link

Use Bit.ly to track click-throughs and create custom short domains and URLs

Using Twitter to help drive traffic to your sites? Measuring that traffic is a smart thing to do. If you have Google Analytics or a similar measuring package, you've got a leg up. But if you don't have access to those tools or the wherewithal to get them set up, or if you want a different take on your data, **use Bit.ly** (http://bit.ly) **for a quick and handy way to track click-throughs.** The example here, which shows that a link Sarah posted received 145 clicks, is just a sliver of what Bit.ly can tell you.

For even more fun, Bit.ly offers a service to shorten URLs under a custom domain like http://nyti.ms (for the *New York Times*) or http://oreil.ly (O'Reilly Media). You don't have to be a fancy company to do this; for example, author Eric Ries has http://ericri.es. (Directions: http://bit.ly/cust-domain.) By the way, the easy-to-read link right there? We created it with Bit.ly's handy one-click URL customizer (as opposed to its *domain* customizer).

twitter tip

Twitter has announced that it will offer a web analytics package to help you track click-throughs and other metrics. As of this writing, it's not yet available, and once it is introduced, we suspect it may appeal mostly to geeks. But keep an eye on the site for its launch and click around once you see it. It could be good stuff.

Help A Reporter Out

@helpareporter New York, NY
http://www.helpareporter.com/

Tweets   Favorites   Following ▾   Followers ▾   Lists ▾

helpareporter Help A Reporter Out
URGHARO: chris.newmarker@finance-commerce.com needs
economic development officials re: Is beer worth economic
development incentives?
11 hours ago

helpareporter Help A Reporter Out
Completed a story thanks to HARO sources or were you quoted?
Post the completed article on our FB fan page: on.fb.me/B6uEG.
11 hours ago

helpareporter Help A Reporter Out
URGHARO: gina@ginaroberts-grey.com needs to know what it
would cost to buy the drugs found in Michael Jackson's room after
he died
13 hours ago

helpareporter Help A Reporter Out
URGHARO: jmulvey@techmedianetwork.com do you use an iPad

Engage journalists and PR people

Twitter is home to thousands of journalists, media workers and PR people. If you're looking to get a little exposure for your company, **Twitter can be a great place to connect with these folks.** We gave you a bunch of meaty tips for doing so in Chapter 3; here are a few more:

1. Post great messages. If your Twitter account is a resource in your sector, journalists will trust you quite a bit more. They may even find you through retweets and comments other people make.

2. Follow the media people who cover your sector. Often, they tweet out when they're looking for sources. In addition, following them is a step toward building a relationship—but proceed with caution; they have a lot of people trying to buddy up to them, and they can smell self-interest from miles off. (We're media people ourselves, so we know whereof we speak.)

3. Follow Help A Reporter Out (@helpareporter). The account regularly posts inquiries from reporters looking for sources.

Web 2.0 Expo ✓

@w2e SF, NY, online...

Web 2.0 Expo NY registration is now open! Use code webny11tw to save an additional 20% http://bit.ly /lioTjw

http://web2expo.com

 About @w2e

4,078	36,024	32,726
Tweets	Following	Followers

You are @w2e

Paw Luxury

@PawLuxury

PawLux.com eco-living for the everyday dog - We offer eco-friendly, organic, natural dog products made in the USA. Contact: Bark@PawLux.com

http://www.pawlux.com

 About @PawLuxury

7,471	22,609	25,423
Tweets	Following	Followers

Recent images

Anita Borg Institute

@anitaborg_org Palo Alto, CA

BJ Wishinsky, Communities Program Mgr, Anita Borg Institute for Women & Technology. Follow @ghc for the Grace Hopper Celebration of Women in Computing.

http://anitaborg.org/

 About @anitaborg_org

7,273	4,440	6,917
Tweets	Following	Followers

Recent images · view all

Follow everyone who follows you (almost)

Individuals, including people who tweet in a primarily professional capacity, have a lot of choice in whom and how many accounts they follow, which we discuss in Chapter 1. But *business* accounts have less latitude. Because when somebody follows you, they're saying, "I'm interested in you and maybe in having conversations with you." When you follow them back, **you're sending the same message, which, if they're a customer or potential customer, will probably delight them.** In addition, following back opens the DM channel (described in Chapter 1), which can be key for customer support.

When you don't follow back, you can appear distant, disinterested or arrogant—exactly the opposite of what your organization is likely aiming for on Twitter.

That said, there are pitfalls to following all your followers. First, it takes time (there are third-party programs that will auto-follow for you, though use them with care, as they're the same tools spammers use, and they can get your account flagged on Twitter). Second, you can easily wind up following spammers, porn stars and other people you may not want associated with your company.

If you have time to check out each follower, great. If not, we recommend not sweating it too much and—again, if you're a business account—following back everyone, or just a lot of people, and definitely those who have a problem and may want to DM you. Naturally, you might skip accounts with vulgar names.

By the way, if following everyone means you can't keep on top of important tweets, use one of the tricks described in Chapter 2 to make sure you see high-priority accounts.

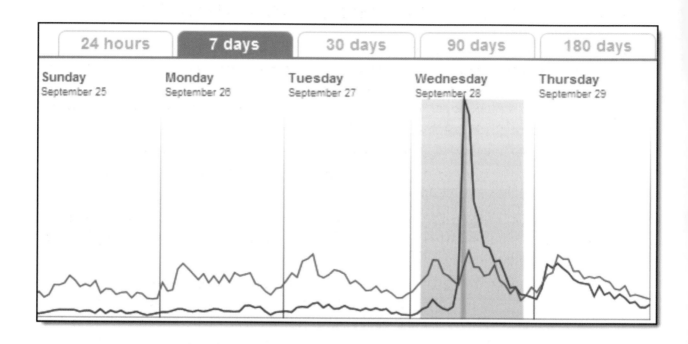

Four services for measuring Twitter

One of the questions businesses ask most often is: **How should we measure Twitter?** That's an impossible question to answer universally, because what you measure—be it volume of retweets, uses of a hashtag, percentage of click-throughs, revenue from coupon code conversions, sentiment of users, or something else altogether—depends entirely on your goals. But a few services can get you started, and these are worth trying:

1. Crowdbooster (http://crowdbooster.com), which provides a suite of analytics, also finds links and content that might be a good fit for your audience, and it tells you the best times to tweet. The service has free and paid options.

2 and 3. RowFeeder (http://rowfeeder.com) and **Sprout Social** (http://sproutsocial.com) both have good reputations for providing some basic free reports and analytics (they both have paid options, too.).

4. Trendistic (http://trendistic.com) lets you compare and graph the incidence of different topics on Twitter (type in your search terms separated by a comma). It's great for getting a sense of whether one idea is more popular than others. The chart here compares "Kindle," the red line, and "iPad," the blue line, during a week that Amazon announced new e-readers and tablets.

Three bonus tools for business accounts

As a business on Twitter, you're likely to need a few **extra-strength tools for analyzing trends, managing your accounts and posting tweets.** In addition to Bit.ly, discussed earlier in this chapter and Chapter 1, here are a handful we like a lot:

1. TweepDiff (http://tweepdiff.com) is a great tool for comparing the followers or followees of your various accounts. It's handy when you're wondering whether there's a big overlap in the constituents for different accounts.

2. CoTweet (http://cotweet.com) is a third-party client designed for corporate use. It's got an array of industrial-strength features to help you manage multiple posters and multiple accounts. Although some people like HootSuite, a similar tool, we don't recommend it because its ht.ly URL shortener breaks the web—instead of redirecting you to the original site, it sends you to a site with a fake ht.ly URL, thereby capturing all of the traffic and the links that search engines love.

3. SocialFlow (http://socialflow.com) is a service that analyzes your audience and then, at optimal times, posts tweets that you've cued up. It's in limited beta (meaning they're in a test phase with a small number of users), but early reports are positive, and it might be worth signing up to try it out.

Thanks for **helping and inspiring** us on this edition: @101cookbooks, @aaker, @acroll, @adamwitwer , @amyjokim, @andrewsavikas, @anildash, @ariannahuff, @backyardbeyond, @baratunde, @benioff, @berginobaseball, @bethkanter, @bjfogg, @bonniedone, @borthwick, @brady, @briansawyer, @carlmalamud, @chrisbrogan, @cookingforgeeks, @corybooker, @crystal, @danmil, @digiphile, @doctorow, @dontgetcaught, @dooce, @ebertchicago, @ediefr , @elonjames, @ericries, @finiteattention, @fredwilson, @ftrain, @gnat, @goodappetite, @griner, @hannahmw23, @harryallen, @heymarci, @hmason, @jamesbuck, @jamilsmith, @jdbookbinder, @jenbee, @jennydeluxe, @jimog, @jkrums, @joshmilstein , @jstogdill, @kabbenbok, @karensatoreilly , @katmeyer, @kati, @katiecouric, @kcpike, @kenyatta, @kimseverson, @lauraklein, @lowflyingrocks, @mai, @marcprecipice, @marshallk, @marthastewart, @mharrisperry, @mkapor, @nancyfranklin, @naypinya, @nmsanchez, @padmasree, @peretti, @petermeyers, @petersagal, @pogue, @pourmecoffee, @prnewswire, @profblmkelley, @putthison, @randomdeanna, @RepsLuvGov, @sarawinge, @sgdean, @simonpegg, @sree, @stephenfry, @susanorlean, @tamyho, @tarasophia, @tayari, @the_real_shaq , @thebostonshaker, @tonystubblebine, @veen, @whitneyhess, @wordnik, @xenijardin, @yasminerashidi, @zephoria, @zoecello, @zoefinkel

Continuing the conversation— and taking a break from it

We want to have a conversation with you about new uses of Twitter and questions you may have. Post comments using the hashtag #TwitterBook, and make sure to include at least one of our @usernames: @timoreilly and @SarahM. If we can't answer a question, look to **Mashable** (http://mashable.com) or **ReadWriteWeb** (http://readwriteweb.com), two of the best sites covering social media, often with how-tos.

Continued conversations aside, **we do recommend that you take occasional breaks from Twitter and other social media.** Our brains are wired to get a small, positive jolt from each new incoming message, and the feeling of connection can be a bit addictive, especially when those messages arrive by the dozen every hour. Indeed, lots of people of find that once they've tapped into social media, they can have a hard time concentrating on other things that *don't* generate constant dopamine hits.

A good way to mitigate the problem is by taking Twitter holidays. A few options:

1. Ignore the site except for, say, thirty minutes at 9 a.m. and 4:30 p.m. every day.

2. Observe a Sabbath and stay offline one day a week.

3. Go on vacation for a week or three a year and leave social media behind.

Your mileage may vary, but getting away from Twitter makes it all the more interesting when you return.

Happy tweeting.

INDEX

Symbols

@ symbol 21, 47, 49, 151, 173, 193
@mentions (see @messages)
@messages 47, 107, 125, 127, 139, 141, 143, 151, 153, 217
@replies (see @messages)
symbol (see Hashtags)
#fb (see Facebook)
#FF (see FollowFriday)
#FollowFriday (see FollowFriday)
#TwitterBook 3, 244
140-character limit 7, 21, 35, 37, 39, 51, 119, 147, 157
140it 37
20x200 223

A

Aaker, Jennifer 171
Adobe Air 93
advanced search 67, 69, 79, 123
advertising on Twitter 229
Allen, Harry 111
ambient awareness 9, 181
ambient intimacy 9, 181
analytics 241

answering questions 123
API 89
Armstrong, Heather 165
asking questions 121, 131
Atherton, Chris 27
authentication 89
auto-DMs 137, 139
avatar (see icon)

B

backgrounds 191
backing up tweets 75
Baldwin, Micah 173
Below, Curtis 127
Benioff, Marc 209
BerginoBaseball 207
bio 27, 189, 191, 211, 213, 215
Bit.ly 39, 177, 179, 235, 241
BlackBerry 95
blocking 61, 139, 145
blogs 155, 157, 197, 225
Booker, Cory 17, 67
bookmarks (see favorites)
Borthwick, John 141
Brogan, Chris 27
Buck, James 105

C

cc'ing 127, 215
celebrities on Twitter 17
cell phone (see Mobile)
Charity: water 171
chronological order, reading tweets in 91, 93
click-throughs, tracking 39, 177, 179, 235
clients (see Third-party clients)
CloudMagic 77
Comcast 165, 211, 221
contests 227
conferences 163, 197
conversation 43, 47, 125, 131, 201, 217
co-presence 181
CoTweet 213, 242
Couric, Katie 159
cross-posting to other sites 193
Crowdbooster 241
custom short domains 235
custom URLs 235
customer feedback, giving 165
customer service 5, 17, 165, 203, 205, 211, 221, 231, 239

D

desktop clients (see third-party clients)
direct messages (see DM)
directories 97
DMs 51, 139, 205, 221, 239
Doctorow, Cory 165
DoesFollow 133
DonorsChoose.org 219
DragonFly Effect, The 171
Dunn, Brian J. 209

E

EasyChirp 19
Echofon 95
email alerts for search terms 73
email delivery of direct messages 47
email notification of followers 29, 133
email signature files 197
enterprise status updates 199
Evans, Meryl K. 131

245

F

Fab 217
Facebook 43, 91, 113, 157, 193, 205
Fail Whale 57
family and friends, keeping track of 101
favorites 87, 175
Favstar 175
Find Friends 29
finding a job 147
Finkel, Zoe 145
Flickr 157, 161, 175
Flipboard 85
followers 99, 105, 129, 133, 155, 225, 227, 229, 233, 239, 241
FollowFriday 43
following 7, 23, 25, 29, 41, 51, 97, 101, 105, 127, 129, 131, 133, 151, 227, 237, 239
Food52 233
Foursquare 141, 157, 195
frequency (see how often to tweet)
FriendOrFollow 133
fundraising 171

G

Get Satisfaction 61
goals, for business accounts 203

Goldberg, Jay 127
Google 75, 83, 153, 165
Google+ 57
Gowalla 195
group chat 131

H

hacked accounts 145
hashtags 3, 43, 53, 55, 79, 131, 163, 173
Hashtags.org 43
help 61, 145
Help A Reporter Out 237
Hipmunk 223
HootSuite 241
how often to tweet 129
HowOftenDoYouTweet 129
Howard, Alex 127
HT 111, 115, 119
https 27
hub-and-spoke model 157
Huffington, Arianna 209
humor 117, 175, 185

I

icon 27, 187, 211
individual messages, linking to 159
influence 99
Instagram 161
internal status updates 199
iPhone 95

J

JetBlue 215
journalists 13, 69, 127, 223, 237
Just Food 223

K

Kanter, Beth 171
Kelley, Blair 151
Kickstarter 171
Kim, Amy Jo 191
Kirkpatrick, Marshall 91
Klout 99, 141
Krums, Janis 13

L

LinkedIn 193
linking to individual messages 159
linking to the web 153, 155, 225
links to your website, tracking 81
Lists 29, 97, 101, 113, 215
Listorious 97
listening (see Twitter search)
live events, tracking 79
live-tweeting 45, 163
location 27, 67, 69, 195
Lu, Yiying 57

M

m.twitter.com 95
making money on Twitter 227
Mashable 244
Maytag 165
measurement 241
Messages (see DMs)
Meyer, Kat 23
misattribution 119
mobile clients 95, 161
mobile set-up (SMS) 33
mobile Twitter (m.twitter.com) 95
mobile updates 33, 95
Monitter 79
MT 111, 115, 119
multiple accounts, coordinating 215
multiple posters on one account 213
Museum of Modern Art 219
muting 91, 129

N

networking 23, 47
news 11-13, 85
News.me 85
non-profits 171, 199
Notifications 29, 47, 51, 133
Novogratz, Jacqueline 209

O

OAuth (see authentication)
OH (overheard) 167
Omnivore Books 233
O'Neal, Shaquille 7, 21
Orlean, Susan 43
overheard 167

P

Paper.li 141
ParaTweet 163
parody accounts 159
PeerIndex 99
phone (see mobile)
picture (see icon)
photos, posting 13, 149, 161
Ping.fm 193
Please retweet 117, 179
Plexus Engine 97, 99
Pogue, David 27
PostPost 77
PR Newswire 213
private accounts 27, 101
profile, how to fill out 25, 27, 187, 189, 211, 213
Promoted Accounts 229
Promoted Trends 229
Promoted Tweets 65, 229
promotions 227
protected accounts 27, 101
publishing 169
Pulse 85

Q

questions (see answering questions, asking questions)
quoting a tweet 91, 111, 113, 115, 119

R

ReadWriteWeb 244
Reichel, Leisa 9
reposting tweets 179
ReSearch.ly 75
Retweet button 111, 113, 115, 193
Retweeting, retweets 49, 109-119, 127, 155, 215, 219
Ries, Eric 191, 195, 235
RowFeeder 241
RSS feeds to Twitter 225
RT (see retweets)

S

sales 227
saved searches 71
scheduling tweets 91, 93, 169, 177
search (see Twitter search)
search alerts (see email alerts, Twitter search)
Search contacts 29
Seesmic 91, 95

Selective Twitter Status 193
Settings 27, 33, 51, 133, 145, 191, 211
Severson, Kim 13
Shirky, Clay 143
shortened URLs (see URL shorteners)
signing messages 213
signing up 21
Smith, Andy 171
SMS (see also text)
SMS short codes 33
SocialFlow 242
SocialOomph 169, 177
Social-search 141
Snapbirg 77
spam 91, 99, 105, 107, 137-143
Sprout Social 241
Srenivasan, Sree 151, 191
Stellar 175
Stewart, Martha 209
Storify 159
Stubblebine, Tony 145
Summify 141
support (see help)
suspended accounts 145

T

t.co 39
text commands 33
text-messaging rates 33
text updates 33, 101

The New York Times 13, 99, 197, 215, 235
third-party clients 37, 79, 89, 91, 93, 95, 161, 169, 177, 193, 213, 241
timeline 45
Topsy 75, 81, 119
tracking click-throughs 39, 177, 179, 235
tracking family and friends 101
tracking links 81
tracking live events 79
transliteration 91
trending topics 15, 53, 59, 83, 229
Trendistic 83, 241
Trends (see trending topics)
Tumblr 157
TweepDiff 242
tweet 45
TweetBackUp 75
TweetBrain 121
TweetChat 131
TweetDeck 79, 93, 95
TweetGrid 79, 131
TweetMeme 85
TweetStats 207
tweetup 55
Twestival 171
Twilert 73

Twitaholic 99
Twitalyzer 99
TwitBacks 191
Twitpic 161
Twitter Analytics 235
Twitter Facebook App 193
Twitter for Android 95
Twitter for BlackBerry 95
Twitter holidays 244
Twitter for iPad 95
Twitter for iPhone 95
Twitter help 61
Twitter search (see also
    advanced search) 15,
    29, 43, 53, 65, 71,
    77, 97, 123, 131,
    201, 221, 229
Twitterific 95
Twopular 83
Twtvite 53

U

unfollowing 135, 143
UberSocial 95
UPS 165
URL shorteners 39, 153
  Retweets, and 119
  to track click-throughs 221
username
  how to pick 21
  promoting 197
Utopic.me 141

V

Verified accounts, 159
via 111, 115, 119
Vimeo 175
Virgin America 219

W

Warrior, Padmasree 209
WeFollow 97
WhatTheTrend 43, 83
when to post 177, 241,
    242
Who To Follow 29, 31
widgets 155, 197

Y

Yammer 199
YFrog 161
YouTube 157, 175

Z

Zandt, Deanna 139, 219
Zarrella, Dan 117
Zite 85
Zscaler 39